PENETRATION TESTI

BCS, THE CHARTERED INSTITUTE FOR IT

BCS, The Chartered Institute for IT, is committed to making IT good for society. We use the power of our network to bring about positive, tangible change. We champion the global IT profession and the interests of individuals, engaged in that profession, for the benefit of all.

Exchanging IT expertise and knowledge
The Institute fosters links between experts from industry, academia and business to promote new thinking, education and knowledge sharing.

Supporting practitioners
Through continuing professional development and a series of respected IT qualifications, the Institute seeks to promote professional practice tuned to the demands of business. It provides practical support and information services to its members and volunteer communities around the world.

Setting standards and frameworks
The Institute collaborates with government, industry and relevant bodies to establish good working practices, codes of conduct, skills frameworks and common standards. It also offers a range of consultancy services to employers to help them adopt best practice.

Become a member
Over 70,000 people including students, teachers, professionals and practitioners enjoy the benefits of BCS membership. These include access to an international community, invitations to a roster of local and national events, career development tools and a quarterly thought-leadership magazine. Visit www.bcs.org/membership to find out more.

Further information
BCS, The Chartered Institute for IT,
First Floor, Block D,
North Star House, North Star Avenue,
Swindon, SN2 1FA, United Kingdom.
T +44 (0) 1793 417 424
F +44 (0) 1793 417 444
(Monday to Friday, 09:00 to 17:00 UK time)
www.bcs.org/contact
http://shop.bcs.org/

PENETRATION TESTING
A guide for business and IT managers

BCS-CREST Penetration Testing Working Party

© BCS Learning & Development Ltd 2019

The right of BCS-CREST Penetration Testing Working Party to be identified as authors of this work has been asserted by them in accordance with sections 77 and 78 of the Copyright, Designs and Patents Act 1988.

All rights reserved. Apart from any fair dealing for the purposes of research or private study, or criticism or review, as permitted by the Copyright Designs and Patents Act 1988, no part of this publication may be reproduced, stored or transmitted in any form or by any means, except with the prior permission in writing of the publisher, or in the case of reprographic reproduction, in accordance with the terms of the licences issued by the Copyright Licensing Agency. Enquiries for permission to reproduce material outside those terms should be directed to the publisher.

All trade marks, registered names etc. acknowledged in this publication are the property of their respective owners. BCS and the BCS logo are the registered trade marks of the British Computer Society charity number 292786 (BCS).

Published by BCS Learning and Development Ltd, a wholly owned subsidiary of BCS, The Chartered Institute for IT, First Floor, Block D, North Star House, North Star Avenue, Swindon, SN2 1FA, UK.
www.bcs.org

Paperback ISBN 9781780174082
PDF ISBN 9781780174099
ePUB ISBN 9781780174105
Kindle ISBN 9781780174112

Ebook available

British Cataloguing in Publication Data.
A CIP catalogue record for this book is available at the British Library.

Disclaimer:
The views expressed in this book are of the authors and do not necessarily reflect the views of the Institute or BCS Learning and Development Ltd except where explicitly stated as such. Although every care has been taken by the authors and BCS Learning and Development Ltd in the preparation of the publication, no warranty is given by the authors or BCS Learning and Development Ltd as publisher as to the accuracy or completeness of the information contained within it and neither the authors nor BCS Learning and Development Ltd shall be responsible or liable for any loss or damage whatsoever arising by virtue of such information or any instructions or advice contained within this publication or by any of the aforementioned.

Publisher's acknowledgements
Reviewers: Ian Glover, Ken Munro, David Jakes, Ciaran Durnin, Chris Frost, Wendy Goucher, Indunil Hettiarachchi, John Hughes, David King, Robert J. Lockwood, Tim Parker, Malcolm Pell and Mike Sheward
Publisher: Ian Borthwick
Commissioning editor: Rebecca Youé
Production manager: Florence Leroy
Project manager: Sunrise Setting Ltd
Copy-editor: Gillian Bourn
Proofreader: Sarah Cook
Indexer: John Silvester
Cover design: Alex Wright
Cover image: Eric Isselee
Typeset by Lapiz Digital Services, Chennai, India

CONTENTS

LIST OF FIGURES AND TABLES

ABOUT THE AUTHORS

Jason Charalambous is an experienced penetration tester, leading technical offensive operations teams. In his role he is responsible for helping organisations to identify weaknesses in order to improve their security posture and to enable them to defend against evolving threats. Jason has years of experience within the industry and previously held roles in implementing information security and compliance practices across organisations.

Ceri Charlton CITP is a former CISO and now Associate Director at Bridewell Consulting. Ceri has worked across information security in a number of both technical and leadership roles. As a consultant, he has investigated and managed the remediation of breaches and applied this knowledge to his own security testing. Ceri has performed application security testing for credit and debit payment systems, discovering previously undetected vulnerabilities within production systems and assisting developers and system owners in closing these. As a CISO, he has also used the services of many third-party penetration testers.

Roderick Douglas has been working at Sheffield Hallam University since 1989, as a network manager, consultant and lecturer. As Network Manager he was involved in the early deployment of Local Area Networks at Sheffield Hallam University and the connection to JANET, the Joint Academic NETwork. Working as a consultant for part of the university delivering commercial and professional IT courses, Roderick delivered training on Novell, Cisco and Microsoft products holding certifications from these organisations. He also developed training materials on wireless networking, web programming and virtualisation. In the Department of Computing Roderick has undertaken both undergraduate and postgraduate academic programme development and delivery, and has received 'Inspirational Teaching' awards from the Faculty. In addition to his roles at Sheffield Hallam University he has given presentations and training on Digital Forensic Analysis for law enforcement in Nigeria through the United Nations Office on Drugs and Crime, and has been a technical reviewer of a Cisco CCNA Networking Academy Publication. Roderick appreciates the proximity of Sheffield to the Peak District, enjoying regular walking, running, cycling and swimming.

Rob Ellis CISSP MBCS is an experienced information security professional whose career has taken him through a wide range of sectors and he is also a regular attendee at industry and BCS security events. Rob's experience working with commercial, defence and government organisations has enabled him to develop practical approaches to meeting the demanding regulatory and compliance requirements faced by organisations today. His capabilities for delivering services securely stem from his background in designing, implementing and supporting infrastructure and application environments.

Rob specialises in delivering vulnerability and penetration test management as part of organisational strategy towards meeting regulatory and organisational security requirements.

Nick Furneaux has been working with and programming computers since being given a Sinclair ZX81 at the age of 12. (At the age of 14 he designed a computer program to convince his teacher that he had gained access to his bank account.) In the past 25 years, he has provided cyber security and digital forensics consultancy for companies and law enforcement institutions in the UK, across Europe, the USA and Asia and has lectured on the subject to numerous organisations. In 2018 he wrote *Investigating Cryptocurrencies*, currently the only book available dealing with the practical challenges and methods for investigating crimes involving cryptocurrency coins. His world-class course on the subject has been studied by hundreds of investigators in the past 12 months. Nick is currently working with and training law enforcement, intelligence and corporate personnel throughout the world in various forms of digital forensic investigations including advanced open-source intelligence-gathering techniques, cryptocurrency crime and RAM analysis.

Sharif Gardner is a cybersecurity consultant and training professional within the cyber insurance sector. He is responsible for providing cyber risk counsel to underwriting teams across a global network, as well as to brokers and clients. He is certified by GCHQ, one of the three intelligence and security agencies in the UK, as a cyber trainer and has developed GCHQ-accredited broker and risk manager programmes. Sharif regularly runs multi-sector crisis management workshops internationally for S&P100 companies. He previously headed up the first fully immersive Cyber Academy in the UK for PGI and oversaw the design, delivery and accreditation of all training globally. Sharif is a renowned speaker at cyber-security and insurance events and contributor to news outlets. Sharif is a former Royal Marine and is credited with authoring the globally recognised Frontier Risks SRMC™, a leading security education programme which provides 60 credits to the University of the West of Scotland's MBA Risk and Resilience programme.

James Hayes is an independent editor and technology writer specialising in enterprise ICT. He contributes to *Cyber Security Europe*, *InfoSecurity Professional* and *Cloud Security*, and was a contributor to *Cyber Terrorism & Ransomware* (Greenhaven Publishing, 2018). Hayes authored the ground-breaking report on risk perspectives for connected vehicles, *Automotive Cyber Security*, in 2015.

Jims Marchang completed his PhD from the CSCAN Research Laboratory, Plymouth University, UK. He is the course leader of Cyber Security at Sheffield Hallam University. He is a member of the Institute of Electrical and Electronics Engineers (IEEE), IEEE young professionals, IEEE internet of things (IoT) community and a Fellow of the Higher Education Academy (HEA), UK. As a researcher, he has published 19 scientific research papers in leading journals and conferences (IEEE, Elsevier, Springer, among others) in the field of networks and security. He is the author of a book called *Optimising Application Performance in Ad Hoc Networks*, a research perspective (2017). He is a reviewer of *IEEE Transactions on Vehicular Technology*, *Heliyon Journal* (Elsevier), *Ad-Hoc Networks* (Elsevier), *Journal of Information Security and Applications* (Elsevier) and *International Journal of Electrical and Computer Engineering*. His current research focuses on blockchain technology and IoT securities.

Gemma Moore is an expert in penetration testing and simulated targeted attack. Having been a CHECK Team Leader since 2007, she holds CREST certifications in Infrastructure, Applications and Simulated Attack. Gemma has spent more than a decade working in the security consultancy industry and has helped customers across a wide range of industry sectors assess their risks and improve their security. Gemma is an engaging presenter and trainer who is passionate about helping her customers improve their own skills and experience. She delivers training and workshops to industry professionals, developers, operational teams and end-users. In recognition of her outstanding level of commitment to the technical information security industry and the highest level of excellence in CREST examinations, Gemma was selected to receive a CREST Fellowship award in 2017.

Tylor Robinson is a graduate security consultant, a pen tester and a tinkerer currently residing in South Africa. When not protecting clients from breaches, he spends his time writing pentesting tools, taking systems apart or learning more about the field. As a result, he has collected a small army of certificates and strives to expand them even more. He would like to use this opportunity to thank his parents, his colleague (you know who you are) and MWR Infosecurity for presenting him with the opportunity to continue working in this field. Now entering his 6th year in the field, he quickly realised that the field is vast and that security is often about more than just the controls. 'It took me a while to break out of my technical shell but I think I've finally got it: Security controls often fail, because there is a lack of understanding, which leads to a lack of support from upper management.' This realisation is the motivation behind contributing to this book. Tylor hopes that this book breaks this stereotype by targeting management and equipping them with the needed pentesting knowledge to effectively drive their security staff.

Felix Ryan grew up among second-hand computers and quickly gained the desire to explore their capabilities. He self-taught BASIC programming and went on to enjoy testing 'technical boundaries' at school. All too slowly, after starting a small web development company he realised that making web apps was not his calling, no matter how securely built they were. Following this realisation, Felix became the security engineer for a boutique cloud consultancy firm that allowed him to specialise in defending infrastructure. He started a part-time MSc in Software and System Security at the University of Oxford and moved to become a junior penetration tester at a growing security consultancy. There he was given a wide range of opportunities including gaining soft consultancy skills as an ISO 27001 Lead Auditor, a Payment Card Industry Qualified Security Assessor (PCI QSA) and gained a distinction in his degree. Risk and compliance work was never Felix's favourite and this was soon replaced by taking greater responsibility within the penetration testing team. Within a short time he rose through the ranks to become the acting team manager. To avoid becoming a member of middle management he traded in his company credit card to become a freelance consultant penetration tester. Today, Felix finds satisfaction working with any organisation interested in pushing itself to do better, and by contributing to the security community.

Peter Taylor CISSP CISM CITP is a Security and Data Protection Officer at UK Asset Resolution. He has over 30 years' experience in information systems, encompassing development, project management and information security, with the majority of these as an information security practitioner in the finance sector. Peter is responsible for data protection, cyber security and information management as part of the risk management team in a major publicly owned UK lending business. He has current and previous experience in developing policies and in their promotion and education for a professional workforce. Peter's career has included defining and operating security controls for a wide range of application systems, including payment technologies, network security systems, mobile and internet applications. He holds a Business honours degree (Bradford University) and a Master's degree in Computer Applications from Cranfield University. Peter is a member of ISC2, ISACA, IAPP and BCS.

Moinuddin Zaki, CISSP, CEH and an AWS Certified Solution Architect, is a security engineer and a seasoned technologist with broad experience in infrastructure engineering and cyber security, based in London, UK. Zaki has a BEng from Bangalore, India and holds an MS in Computing and Security from King's College London. Zaki is passionate about security engineering, DevSecOps, cloud security and penetration testing.

FOREWORD

In the last few years, we have experienced cyber-crime on a scale never seen before and an unprecedented increase in threat actors. It has been a wake-up call for all businesses and organisations to take cyber security seriously and discover where their weaknesses lie and how to fix them before someone else finds and exploits them. The best way to do this is to simulate malicious attacks – the art of penetration testing. While penetration testing has traditionally been associated with government organisations and large financial institutions and corporations, it is now commonplace among medium sized companies, NGOs and the wider public and private sector.

That's why this book is so important. Penetration testing is extremely sensitive, complex and skilled work and requires a deep understanding of how to plan, manage and get the maximum benefits from a testing programme. There is also the question of trust. The buying community needs to have confidence in its service providers, and professionally qualified individuals with the processes and methodologies to protect data and integrity.

BCS and the book's working group have gone to great lengths to research the industry and have drawn on the knowledge and experience of some of the UK's leading penetration testers and cyber security experts. The book provides valuable advice and guidance from start to finish for all parties involved in the process and highlights the implications of new regulations such as GDPR.

CREST is a not-for-profit accreditation and certification body that was set up in 2006 to help deliver a more professionalised penetration testing industry in the UK. Today it has members all over the world with a focus on multiple other disciplines as well as penetration testing. This growth demonstrates the increasingly vital role that penetration testing now has in protecting data, systems and critical infrastructure. I would recommend that anyone wanting to learn more about penetration testing reads this book.

Ian Glover, President, CREST

ABBREVIATIONS

API	application programming interface
AUP	acceptable use policy
BYOD	bring your own device
CAPEC	Common Attack Pattern Enumeration and Classification scheme
CD	continuous delivery
CDE	cardholder data environment
CI	continuous integration
CIA	confidentiality, integrity, availability
CIO	chief information officer
CISO	chief information security officer
CMDB	configuration management database
COO	chief operations officer
CREST	Council for Registered Ethical Security Testers
CVE	Common Vulnerabilities and Exposures
CVSS	Common Vulnerability Scoring System
CWE	Common Weakness Enumeration
DC	data centre
DoS	denial of service
FIM	file integrity monitoring
GDPR	General Data Protection Regulation
GRC	governance, risk and compliance
HIPAA	Health Insurance Portability and Accountability Act
HVAC	heating, ventilation and air conditioning
ICO	Information Commissioner's Office
IEEE	Institute of Electrical and Electronics Engineers
IP	intellectual property
IPS	intrusion prevention system
ISMS	information security management system
ISO	International Organization for Standardization
ITSM	IT service management

NCSC	National Cyber Security Centre
NOC	network operations centre
OLA	operational level agreement
ONR	Office for Nuclear Regulation (UK)
OSSTMM	Open Source Security Testing Methodology Manual
OWASP	Open Web Application Security Project
PCI DSS	Payment Card Industry Data Security Standard
PCI QSA	Payment Card Industry Qualified Security Assessor
QSA	qualified security assessors
RA	risk assessment
RACI	responsible, accountable, consulted and informed, in reference to stakeholders
RFID	radio-frequency identification
RFP	request for proposals
SaaS	software as a service
SCADA	supervisory control and data acquisition
SDLC	software development lifecycle
SLA	service level agreement
SOC	security operations centre
SQL	Structured Query Language
VM	virtual machine
VOIP	voice over internet protocol
VPN	virtual private network
WAF	web application firewall

GLOSSARY

Attack vector: An entry route into a system.

Black-box testing: Implies the tester has no knowledge of the system under test.

Compliance standards: The framework of requirements set out by government, regulatory bodies and other organisations.

Cyber attack: A modern colloquial term meaning the accessing, or blocking, of a digital asset such as a computer, device or an entire network by a person or group, without permission of the owner.

Fingerprinting: The act of gathering certain attributes of a computer or person and drawing conclusions from that data to help make an attack more successful. Also known as 'profiling'.

Grey-box testing: Provides the tester with some internal knowledge of the system under test.

Hacker: A technically skilled person who attempts to subvert the intended functionality of a device or system. In the context of information security, this often means attacking a digital asset.

Information assurance: The processes required to provide confidence in the capabilities of an organisation's information systems to protect information.

Information governance: The organisational approach taken to meet regulatory, legal and risk requirements delivered through a system of policies, procedures and controls.

Man-in-the-middle attack: In cryptography and computer security, a man-in-the-middle attack (MITM) is an attack where the attacker intercepts, relays and possibly alters the communications between two parties or systems which assume they are communicating directly with each other.

Phishing: An attempt to coerce a person to act in a way beneficial to an attacker. This is a social engineering attack. This may be by phone, email or other means.

Red Teaming: A type of test where testers use expertise, guile and techniques such as profiling of their target and social engineering to develop a sophisticated threat 'package', which is used in an attempt to circumvent installed security controls.

Regulatory bodies: Government or industry bodies charged with ensuring that organisations are operating in an appropriate manner.

Spear phishing: A targeted attack against a specific individual or company.

White-box testing: Full knowledge of the system under test is provided to the tester in advance.

PREFACE

James Hayes, Editor

This book provides managers with responsibility for the information security of organisations with the knowledge they need to establish, and derive most value from, penetration test programmes.

The book is aimed at managers who work both in business and in IT functions, and is designed to serve as a common point of reference for both perspectives so that they can be aligned in their understanding of the issues and challenges of penetration test oversight. Penetration testing should ideally be a shared responsibility between IT operations and business operations, as part of a holistic enterprise cyber-security strategy.

Cyber security is a high-profile topic for organisations of all descriptions. Our dependency on networked IT systems has been challenged by the rise of malicious forces that seek to gain unlawful access to those systems, and the data they hold. To counter this, IT security has become a defining dynamic in the conduct of digital business, and in the discharge of executive diligence.

As more organisations have become exposed to cyber threats, cyber security has become a C-suite-level concern; and now other stakeholders – business partners, shareholders and regulators – want assurance that cyber-defences are tested and strengthened throughout organisations they work with.

Changes to data governance laws – such as GDPR (General Data Protection Regulation) – also mean that organisations must have in place cyber-security processes to safeguard data assets and to protect their systems' operational integrity.

These factors make penetration testing increasingly a business issue. Managers with responsibility at all levels within the organisation must therefore understand what penetration testing is, why penetration tests are important and how to procure them. Ideally, they should also know how they can actively support their penetration testers.

Penetration testers probe and audit the security of enterprise IT systems by replicating – in a controlled programme – the penetrative techniques used by cyber attackers. By doing so in a programmatic and methodological way, they identify vulnerabilities, assess risk levels they represent and report them to business owners who decide remedial actions to take.

As a result, business owners and other enterprise managers have to be involved on the client side of the penetration test decision-making process. This means non-technical managers – such as sales people, finance controllers, product developers and human resource (HR) supervisors – need guidance that explains concepts in non-technical terms, and that will educate them sufficiently to be able to engage with IT and non-IT management.

By the same token, IT professionals with an understanding of security products and deployment may have limited experience of penetration test techniques and want to deepen their understanding before they work with penetration testers.

This publication meets these complementary information requirements. Primarily, the target readership are business and IT managers and professionals responsible for setting information security strategy and implementing penetration testing. This book will also be of interest to those in roles such as non-executive directors, governance officers, financial directors, facilities managers and line managers, and may also benefit those interested in a career as a penetration tester, cyber-security specialist or IT professional.

The book has been authored by a team of industry and academic practitioners, including penetration test experts, consultants, technology researchers and theorists, and end-users, in association with CREST, an accreditation body. CREST 'serves the needs of a technical information security marketplace that requires the services of a regulated professional services industry' and 'provides organisations with confidence that the penetration test services they buy will be carried-out by qualified individuals with up-to-date knowledge, skill and competence of the latest vulnerabilities and techniques used by real attackers'.[1]

The authors' rationale has been to:

1. Introduce readers to penetration testing concepts and practices, aims and objectives.

2. Broadly explain the reasons why penetration tests are important to organisational governance and leadership.

3. Explain the issues and challenges that organisations looking to be tested should consider.

4. Outline basic technological points that have a bearing on, or are affected by, penetration testing.

5. Explain how penetration test services should be researched, assessed and procured.

6. Provide basic understanding of penetration testing procedures, methods and applications.

7. Give tested organisations guidance that helps them evaluate possible courses of action once a penetration test report has been delivered.

It is the authors' hope that this publication will serve as a valuable addition to the growing range of defensive tools available to managerial professionals who must now play a part in safeguarding our valuable data. We hope also that its contents provide enlightening and insightful reading along the way.

The following icons have been used throughout the book:

 Anecdote

 Case Study

 Danger

 Definition

 Golden Rule

 Hints/Tips

 Ideas

1 WHAT IS PENETRATION TESTING?

Nick Furneaux

In the mid-15th century BC the Old Testament (Hebrew) Bible describes the wandering of the Israelite people who had purportedly been released from Egyptian bondage by Divine hand. Some 70 years later they stood on the edge of the so-called 'Promised Land', waiting to wage war on the peoples within. But before any attack, the patriarchal leader Moses ordered the first 'penetration test' I could locate in recorded history. In simple terms, Moses sent in spies to test out the defences of the land. This is what they reported to Moses (*Numbers* 13:27):

> We entered the land into which you sent us, and it is indeed flowing with milk and honey, and this is its fruitage. Nevertheless, the people who dwell in the land are strong, and the fortified cities are very great. We also saw the Anakim there … and the Canaanites are dwelling by the sea and along the Jordan.

This was, by any definition, an aggressive, well-planned penetration test. Their mission was to test the ability to penetrate the defences of the target and the test successfully highlighted a number of positive opportunities and also issues for them to address:

- The target was asset rich, metaphorically 'flowing with milk and honey'. This meant that there were high-value goods to be captured making it worth the effort to attack.
- Fortified cities. The defences were strong.
- They 'fingerprinted' the peoples, their locations and strengths.

Fingerprinting is a term used when planning both technical and social engineering type attacks. It is the act of gathering certain attributes of a computer or person and drawing conclusions from that data to help make an attack more successful. A more common term used when gathering data on individuals is 'profiling'.

This metaphor demonstrates exactly the elements that make up the purpose and the desired results of an 'aggressive' penetration test against an organisation's technical and personnel infrastructure. To deploy technical measures, to discover high-value targets, to fingerprint the defences and identify vulnerable resources which need to be exploited to gain access to, or perhaps destroy, the high-value elements.

HOW DOES THIS AFFECT MY ORGANISATION?

Every company, organisation or agency has their 'milk and honey', something worth stealing, exploiting or destroying, and it is fundamentally the steps taken by Moses that an attacker would employ to attack your business. An attacker would ask the following questions:

1. Does your organisation have something I want to exploit, steal or destroy?
   a. information;
   b. intellectual property;
   c. money;
   d. reputation;
   e. conduit to another business with any of the above.
2. What are the defences in place to protect these assets?
   a. Can I potentially attack or circumvent the defences?
   b. Can I coerce, bribe or otherwise leverage an employee?
3. Once inside your network, what can I expect, what can I do, how do I get to my target?

The problem is that we all tend to see our business or organisation in the paradigm of what it makes, sells, employs or otherwise. We do not naturally look at it as an attacker would. For example, your organisation may value its customer list and see risk in terms of what a competitor could do with it. However, an attacker may instead see a customer list as an opportunity to use the data to carry out identity theft, use bank details to steal money, sell stored credit card details and many other possibilities. Indeed, the result of a successful hack may have losses that were not as easy to foresee.

A cyber attack, otherwise known as a 'hack', is a modern colloquial term meaning the accessing of a digital asset such as a computer, device or an entire network by a person or group, without permission of the owner. The term hacker used to have a positive connotation, relating to a computer programmer or engineer, but has changed in the last 20 years to mean a person who would attempt to attack a digital asset for a variety of reasons.

A good example of this was the cyber attack against the mobile and broadband operator TalkTalk in October 2015 (Hodge, 2016). Considerable sums are spent by the company every year protecting the mobile and internet networks it operates and ensuring that private call data is safe from attackers. However, the hack against an arguably softer part of the network resulted in the loss of 150,000 customer records; 15,000 of these included bank account details. Interestingly, in this case, there was no suggestion that these details were used to attack individuals, so it may appear that there was no lasting harm done.

Was there a cost to TalkTalk? Its own figures pointed to a loss of 95,000 customers in three months specifically due to the hack, losing the company an estimated £60 million, perhaps more. Was the hack the result of a nation-state attack or the attention of a crime group? No, in 2016 a 17-year-old boy stood trial for the hack, carried out from his bedroom, and was given a 12-month youth rehabilitation order (Burgess, 2016; ITV News, 2016).

The best type of penetration test will not only probe your network but also identify the risks, the 'milk and honey' of your organisation and recommend methods to mitigate loss.

WHY CARRY OUT A PENETRATION TEST?

Your organisation, in fact every organisation, is a target. A small car repair garage could be a target for ransomware, perhaps asked to pay just £100s to unlock data encrypted by malware, which may be a significant sum to a small business. A mid-sized software house may have unreleased software worth stealing; a pharmaceutical company's intellectual property could be worth millions; even a free online forum may contain user data that would be useful or valuable to an attacker. Every organisation has something worth acquiring. Aside from that, an attacker may just access a network and destroy data, simply for the challenge, just because it's there.

Too often we see penetration tests being carried out purely to tick a proverbial box for the company board. It may be that the only motives for having a penetration test carried out are for attaining a security standard, fulfilling a contract or insurance terms or simply because it's the right thing to do. Although these are sound reasons, the primary purpose should be to **fully test** and **understand** vulnerabilities that may exist within your organisation. When a penetration test is done just to 'tick a box', the resulting report is often read (sometimes just the Executive Summary) and filed until next year with often limited action being taken.

An effective penetration test should fully emulate what a prospective attacker would do, results should be considered and where possible, solutions and fixes implemented.

The top three key benefits of penetration testing to businesses, cited by respondents to a BCS penetration survey undertaken in March 2017,[1] were:

- identification of security weaknesses;
- assurance;
- compliance.

Getting proactive

If an attacker is going to ask questions of your network, those responsible for the business need to ask them first. It is concerning to note that in many organisations the task of protecting the organisation from attack falls squarely in the hands of the

IT department. This is the wrong place to start. The board, following consultation with pertinent departments such as IT, legal and compliance, along with key leaders such as the chief information officer (CIO) and chief information security officer (CISO), should first identify the likely business targets and think through the possible risks, from the irritation of adware appearing on computers to the risks that could result in a business-ending event. Those decisions should not just be the domain of IT – part of it, yes – but management should be driving that conversation.

Unless your business has virtually unlimited resources to spend on consultants, the most effective penetration tests are the ones defined by the organisation itself. An external penetration test company will not be able to easily understand the nuances of your business and a board that has thought carefully about the business-affecting risks can more efficiently target a penetration test against the right assets. This does not mean that a penetration test should always be carried out internally, indeed there are arguments against that, but simply that targets are more easily defined by an organisation. Perhaps the best balance is for a business to define and identify its weaknesses and have those tested both internally and by an experienced external resource.

PENETRATION TESTS WON'T ALWAYS STOP YOU BEING HACKED

In 2016, we at CSITech spent three months planning and executing a penetration test attack against a large bank. We were successful, lessons were learned, holes were plugged and defences hardened. A month later the head of international banking received an email from 'CEOofthebank@gmail.com', asking for $2 million to be transferred to an account in the Middle East immediately. So, he paid up. Our penetration test did its job and improvements were made, but we had not accounted for a person who could not identify a badly constructed phishing attack. This highlighted an area for corporate training.

> Phishing. This word indicates an attempt to coerce a person to act in a way beneficial to an attacker. This is a social engineering attack. This may be by phone, email or other means. Usually the word is used when related to an email to many individuals, perhaps asking them to click a malevolent link or respond with information useful to the attacker. A targeted attack against a specific individual is termed a spear-phishing attack.

It is vital that appropriate expectations are set for the board when signing the contract on a penetration test. Penetration testing is a crucial exercise, but it is possible that a test will not highlight an area which is later exploited. Penetration testing can never cover all the bases.

Don't forget the employees

Your organisation undoubtedly has spent significant resources hardening your network. You install firewalls, intrusion detection systems, anti-virus scanners and a host of other technological defences. The problem is that organisations then make the critical 'mistake' of filling the organisation with people. People like to help – but in the security world, that is bad. We train them that way, we tell them that the customer is always right (bad), that you should 'go the extra mile' (also bad).

Now, this is, of course, a facetious view of the subject. We need reception staff to smile and be helpful, we need customer relations to not be suspicious of every phone call and email. However, as with the example above, the vast number of modern attacks against companies start with some type of what is termed a 'social engineering' attack – essentially, manipulating a human rather than a computer to provide them with information that will often make a resulting technical attack easier. Consider some highly simplified examples:

- 'Hello, this is Sam in IT' (it's not). 'Have you changed your password recently? No? Let me talk you through it and help you choose a strong one.'
- 'I wonder what's on this USB key I found on the floor in reception...'
- 'Hello friendly receptionist, I have an interview, but spilt coffee on my CV, could I quickly use your computer to access my email and print a replacement?'
- 'I've got an email with a £50 voucher for my favourite clothes store, I must be on a mailing list, I just have to click this link...'.

It is easy to see how, if professionally done, these examples could work, providing an attacker with network access without ever attacking or hacking your expensive firewall. Many other examples can be found at www.phishing.org/phishing-examples.

Frequently these attacks are the result of internet-based research, often called open-source intelligence gathering, carried out by an attacker to glean vital information that they can use to improve the likely success of a social engineering approach or a direct technical attack.

The hacking group Anonymous coined the term 'doxing', essentially finding all the documents on a person or company.

Your organisation, or a third party, should be looking at what information the company leaks through social media, forums, websites and the like.

Modern penetration testing should always include the testing and training of your staff to detect these types of attacks.

An attacker may want to know what firewall your organisation uses. This can be achieved using technical measures but could be easy to detect. They may use a simple Google search to provide possible answers. For example, perhaps you want to know what firewall technology a company uses. Try typing the following into Google:

5

site:linkedin.com firewall company name

This simple search will just look at entries on the LinkedIn site that contain the words 'firewall' and the name of the company. By clicking a link and looking at persons on LinkedIn can you discern what firewalls are likely in use by looking at the skills of people who work there? Try it with your own organisation – you may be surprised…

STAYING CURRENT WITH EMERGING RISKS

Although crimes such as burglary, fraud, destruction of property and suchlike are as old as civilisation, their application to technology is much more complex. Whereas a property can only be broken into via doors and windows, the ability of an attacker to break into a network shifts and changes with every passing day. Unlike a building, the potential entry points of a network are constantly altering. How so?

A network is a sum of many parts, this could include routers, computers and mobile devices but now extends to the Internet of Things, such as cameras, building control systems, even equipment that controls industrial machinery. Each of those parts contains software and hardware that may be found to be vulnerable to some type of attack. Once a vulnerability is discovered by or disclosed to a hardware or software vendor, they will usually (but not always) move to patch that problem. This corrective measure can, however, result in new vulnerabilities being exposed and the problem continues.

In 2008 in Refahiye, Turkey, an oil pipeline exploded. It was first thought to be an industrial accident until it was discovered that 60 hours of CCTV had been deleted from servers, and a camera on a separate network showed shadowy figures with a laptop snooping around a control box during the night. The investigation showed that control systems had been remotely hacked to increase the pressure in the pipe resulting in an explosion. Were the control systems vulnerable? No, a simple vulnerability in the monitoring CCTV system, which was on the same network as the control systems, was used to tunnel into the critical control infrastructure, resulting in the destruction of the pipeline (Hazardex, 2014).

This shifting 'threat landscape' makes staying up to date with potential risks a complex task. The primary solution is to have robust procedures for patch management. It is likely that your IT team routinely upgrades server and desktop operating systems – indeed, the deployment of these patches is often automated. Automating patch management is controversial: if an update from a software or hardware supplier is flawed or compromised, this could cause other system problems, crashes, compatibility issues with connected devices and so on. Some organisations delay and test updates to ensure that unforeseen problems are minimised; however, conversely, this approach extends the time for an attacker to exploit non-updated code.

However, the same attention is not given to software and firmware patches relating to systems that may slip into a different department's oversight. For example, we regularly see CCTV systems still configured with their default firmware and passwords, even though many patches have been released. The same is true for building control systems, radio-frequency identification (RFID) entry systems and similar. This is often because oversight for the system sits elsewhere from IT and the owners are not security aware. Fundamentally, the technical responsibility for security of **any** system connected to the network should lie within the IT or network security team. Of course, sometimes these systems are maintained and supported by third-party organisations who may not have the same motivation to upgrade and patch systems as your own staff. Risks and benefits need to be balanced when outsourcing support.

Another problem is the long-term issue of support of hardware and software. Manufacturers seem to be increasingly keen to cease development and support of products soon after new versions are released. This can leave assets vulnerable to newly developed attacks.

Also worth considering is that a person bringing a device into work and connecting to the network via a cable or Wi-Fi may introduce an 'invisible' attack vector. A good example of this is employees plugging-in their own wireless router into the company network so that their iPad or another device can access the internet. Often these have default passwords or are mistakenly left without encryption turned on, providing an open door for an attacker who may scan your premises for open Wi-Fi networks.

Another method for a manager to keep up to date with vulnerabilities that could affect their company is by monitoring specialist search engines such as Shodan.[2] Shodan enables a manager to search for devices of interest, and receive a list of known vulnerabilities. This is constantly changing, so searches should be done routinely.

In addition to your own research and policies, any penetration test that is carried out on your network should report not just what you know, but what you do not know. You should be thinking outside of the proverbial box, looking for vulnerabilities that exist using both direct attacks but also considering the lateral approaches that could be employed that you may not have considered.

A good penetration test team will learn about the business and, rather than simply run network scanners and produce automated reports, will strive to identify the areas of risk, the likely threat actors and understand methods that could be employed against you. This should include social engineering attacks as mentioned previously.

WHY ALL MANAGERS SHOULD BE INTERESTED IN SECURITY...

In 1989 Ronald Reagan said 'Information is the oxygen of the modern age. It seeps through the walls topped by barbed wire, it wafts across the electrified borders'.[3] Information pervades every part of an organisation and it is that very information that can be valuable to an attacker but also the fuel by which to launch an attack. As information is generated or used by every department it is beholden on each manager of a department to be security aware to an appropriate degree.

For example, human resources hold significant information on employees and the organisation and the manager should be aware of the risks of mistakenly releasing or losing any of that data, providing appropriate training to their team.

Customer relation teams need to be well trained by their manager in understanding what data is appropriate to share with an external caller. Reception managers should understand policies relating to physical access to the building and what information is appropriate or inappropriate to be shared with a visitor.

All managers need to be aware of security risks and educate their teams to recognise everything from general phishing emails through to well-researched and crafted spear-phishing attempts to extract information or request actions to be taken.

IMPACT ON THE ORGANISATION OF NOT PENETRATION TESTING

Penetration testing can be a time-consuming and reasonably costly process to do properly. It is for these reasons that organisations often sideline this task, instead trusting that IT are doing their job correctly, and that the investment in security hardware and software should do the job fine. This thinking is a false economy – and could cost you dearly. As was previously explained, the cyber-attack surface is an ever-changing environment and both testing internally while also enabling an experienced third party to test your environment is a critical task. Let's consider the risks and likely costs of not penetration testing your organisation.

Indirect risks or costs here include the following:

- Not being security aware, at board, management and employee levels, leaves the company exposed to a range to attacks via technical and social engineering means.

- A serious hack of your business may have to be disclosed due to due-diligence, General Data Protection Regulation (GDPR) reporting or trade body rules. Investors, for example, may ask for disclosure about pre-planning and pre-testing that was done to avoid any loss. If there is little or no pre-testing this can have a detrimental effect on share price. Hence, a hack which actually resulted in no direct financial loss can result in significant loss via the company's share value.

- A loss of information can result in serious reputational damage which could affect suppliers, and existing and potential customers. This is very difficult to quantify ahead of any attack. However, looking at reputational losses from others in your sector can help you to model the potential effects.

- Cost of post-event forensic investigations can be lengthy and expensive. Indeed, a full investigation into a cyber attack can easily cost more than a penetration test. Although security holes may be found and closed, the possibility of detection of a perpetrator resulting in a prosecution is rare unless the police are involved. Sadly, squeezed budgets and resources often mean that the police will only take on cases that are the most high-profile or where there are extensive losses.

Direct risks or costs here include the following:

- **Loss of intellectual property** (IP) can have significant effects. For example, a simple attack against a small pharmaceutical company resulted in the loss of recipe IP for certain health foods it manufactured. The financial losses were undetected for over a year until a company director saw copies of its products for sale during a trip to China. The losses were significant, as selling its legitimate product into the country at much higher prices became impossible. Legal challenges hit constant dead-ends and the failed litigation costs added to the overall losses.

- **Compensation payments** may also need to be made to customers that have had their details stolen. For example, a mobile phone company lost 2 million records in 2012, and although it did not make direct compensation payments to customers, it was directed by the telecoms regulator to provide a two-year subscription to a fraud detection service to each affected person. This cost the company an estimated £20 million.

- **Loss of money**. A cyber attack may take the form of a hack against the network or can be a simple variation of the 'false-invoice' attack. If the accounts system can be penetrated, then false invoices can be inserted and often payment made without any detection. A good example is the account of the bank mentioned earlier in the chapter where a simple email asked for money to be transferred, and it was.

- **Fines from regulators**. If your organisation is regulated by, for example, a telecoms or financial regulator, then it may fine you if it is not satisfied that your pre-attack and post-attack planning and execution was up to standard. For example, the Financial Conduct Authority (FCA) can impose a maximum penalty of £500,000. Since GDPR came into effect in mid-2018 there are also fines that can total €20 million or 4 per cent of international revenue.

Penetration tests alone will not eliminate all the possibilities of a successful cyber attack, but pre-planning, carrying out penetration tests and even role playing the attacker can help to mitigate the effects and costs.

SUMMARY

We have seen that every business has its 'milk and honey' which attackers may want to steal, leverage or destroy. It is vital that the likely targets are clearly identified, protected and then their defences rigorously tested. Although the IT department has the primary technical role of caring for computer-based resources, the role of identifying business-critical targets needs to fall squarely with the board. Hence, multi-departmental collaboration is essential in planning penetration testing, enabling diverse skills and interests to be represented and dealt with appropriately.

An oft-repeated mantra is that 'security is the responsibility of the individual'. This requires all staff being trained in basic security practices and then having that training tested. Skills such as being able to recognise a social engineering attack or a phishing email can stop attacks or technical exploitation of a network right at the point of entry.

Planning, training and collaborative working are the elements needed for a successful security environment.

REFERENCES

Burgess, M. (2016) TalkTalk hack toll: 100k customers and £60m. *Wired*, 2 February 2016. Available at: www.wired.co.uk/article/talktalk-hack-customers-lost

Hazardex (2014) Russian hackers now thought to have caused 2008 Turkish oil pipeline explosion. 21 December 2014. Available at: www.hazardexonthenet.net/article/88497/Russian-hackers-now-thought-to-have-caused-2008-Turkish-oil-pipeline-explosion.aspx

Hodge, N. (2016) TalkTalk's £400,000 data hack fine is a dire warning. *Compliance Week*, 8 November 2016. Available at: https://www.complianceweek.com/talktalks-400000-data-hack-fine-is-a-dire-warning/2879.article

ITV News (2016) Boy, 17, behind massive TalkTalk data hack sentenced to 12-month rehabilitation order. ITV Report, 13 December 2016. Available at: www.itv.com/news/2016-12-13/boy-17-behind-massive-talktalk-data-hack-sentenced-to-12-month-rehabilitation-order/

2 SUCCESSFUL PENETRATION TESTING: AN OVERVIEW

Sharif Gardner

Most people who have worked in a security and risk management environment will understand that keeping up to date with tools, techniques and skills is as much a part of a job in the IT industry as actually doing the job! In the very specific yet evolving world of penetration testing – a method for assessing and managing risk by thinking and acting like an attacker to 'penetrate' a web application, system or network – the various attack vectors (routes in) and vulnerabilities change constantly, and it can be a daunting challenge for security teams and IT managers to maintain a constant state of protection. There are a multitude of reasons why an organisation will penetration test and it has become part of the quality assurance process. Done correctly and for the right reasons, penetration testing can be considered one of the most effective ways of identifying and plugging gaps. Imagine securing your home for instance: we spend time and money on ensuring intruders can't break into our house, with locks on our windows and doors, alarms and intrusion detection systems. However, seldom do we hire an ethical 'burglar' to try to test that by going as far as they can to break in. With that in mind, a good penetration test can exploit weaknesses within an organisation that go beyond what a routine vulnerability scan may produce, such as seeking to exploit weaknesses in employee security awareness or, more commonly, to expose weaknesses in software systems.

This chapter will delve into some of the core concepts surrounding what effective penetration testing looks like and how it is deployed, while demystifying some of the nuances and key differences between terms such as 'vulnerability testing' and 'Red Team testing'.

UNDERSTANDING WHAT PENETRATION TESTING WILL ACHIEVE

Penetration testing is, in effect, a kind of risk discovery and management tool. It is a way of testing the stability and security of IT systems against attacks perpetrated by computer hackers.

Typically, penetration testing employs a series of manual and automated techniques to simulate an attack. The tester attempts to gain access to a network, acting as if no such access has been authorised. Effective testing attacks through several system entry routes or 'attack vectors', often simultaneously.

Penetration tests attempt to find and exploit system vulnerabilities, and to discover weaknesses within IT systems which may derive from poor or improper system configuration, hardware or software flaws, or operational weaknesses. Penetration tests should be run against all external-facing connections and applications.

Testing is usually carried out from the position of a potential real-world threat actor, and it considers what they may hope to achieve in breaching a system.

A threat actor is a malicious hacker with the intent and capabilities to find weaknesses in systems and networks for the purpose of gaining unauthorised access.

While many large companies in sectors such as defence and finance will conduct penetration testing internally, for most, penetration testing is conducted by an independent, qualified (by CREST for instance) penetration testing expert instructed with a carefully considered 'Scope of Works' (the Scope) and often using a scientifically based, repeatable approach (CREST, 2017). Many firms provide this service. Their testers

Tools for the job

Well-funded state-sponsored or government hackers might develop their own exploits (for example, as exposed by WikiLeaks with the release of CIA hacking tools[1]). This is expensive and time-consuming, and serves to only benefit the government which builds them. These exploits are designed to penetrate serious vulnerabilities not known (or disclosed) to manufacturers and are known as 'Zero Day' (sometimes termed '0Day') vulnerabilities. These are particularly problematic and can introduce large-scale systemic risk because they provide a weakness in a particular software system that allows cyber criminals or nation-state actors to control a system or device or deliver malware. Because the vulnerability is undisclosed, this means that every system affected is vulnerable to its spread, quickly causing potential devastation dependent on the payload delivered; a payload being a component of the computer virus that maliciously executes. This can be anything from spam, to a remote access tool, to a destructive malware designed to wipe data.

Tools deployed by penetration testers are the same that criminals will use to gain unauthorised entry in nearly all other instances. The most common tool used by both good and bad sides of the hacking community, is the popular Kali Linux distribution.[2] Various tools are then used within that; for example, Nmap,[3] first released in 1997, which is a network mapping and security auditing tool that will provide anyone using it with critical information on the network inventory. Another is Metasploit,[4] a framework tool for verifying vulnerabilities and developing exploits.

Effectively, Kali Linux comes with a suite of tools that help with information gathering and the deployment of exploit payloads. The tools are the same used by both sides – it is the exploit payloads (malware) that make the difference. If there is a new undiscovered vulnerability within a system, then a well-funded attacker might take great time and effort to write a specific piece of code to breach that system. However, most of the malware used by nefarious hackers (for commoditised or even targeted crimes) and security researchers (penetration testers) is still open-source. It is important to note that Kali Linux and its suite of tools can test the security of any IP-connected device and is not limited to Linux targets.

will deploy exactly the same tools as their nefarious counterparts, to make the test as realistic as possible. Only this approach can test how far actual hackers are able to penetrate networks and systems.

What penetration testing is, and what it is not

Several terms can be conflated with penetration testing. One is 'vulnerability testing' or 'vulnerability scanning', which is **not** the same as penetration testing. Penetration testing differs from vulnerability testing (or scanning) in that the tester will go further than simply uncovering system weaknesses. By behaving like a hacker, the testers will take the next steps to exploit the system's vulnerabilities or overcome security measures – for example, by gaining access to data or simulating the compromise of an organisation's physical security.

Simply put, the key difference between a vulnerability scan and a penetration test is that a vulnerability scan may scan your internal network to compare details about the organisation's attack surface[5] with known Common Vulnerabilities and Exposures (CVE)[6] and security gaps in services and ports, or scan the external network for vulnerabilities. This in itself is generally enough for a low-budget test.

Vulnerability scans use off-the-shelf products to scan IP addresses or IP ranges. A penetration test must be conducted by a skilled tester. A penetration tester will use vulnerability scanning as part of a penetration test and take the output from the scan to then further exploit any vulnerabilities. A well-scoped penetration test will identify the extent of the problem, which requires a level of investigation to identify what type and potentially the volume of information that could be accessed. Penetration testers will use automated tools, but the ability to interpret the responses of the tools is what sets them apart.

Organisations will need to take a risk-based, cost-effective approach to penetration testing and thus organisations with strict budget constraints and that wish to avoid embarking on a penetration testing programme should as a bare minimum carry out vulnerability assessments. This is always the first step an organisation should take at any rate because, as explained, it will highlight any vulnerabilities and will allow the organisation to: (i) validate the corrective action taken to close out known vulnerabilities; and (ii) following a penetration test, identify any vulnerabilities which were not identified during the routine vulnerability scanning.

Vulnerability testing is typically automated, and searches for known vulnerabilities. Critically, penetration tests involve real people who behave like actual skilled hackers. In this way they are unlike automated systems, and go far beyond security compliance testing, which checks if specified security protocols are in place, rather than testing their effectiveness. Vulnerability testing is a very quick process; proper, effective penetration testing may take days or weeks.

There are some good practices that organisations should adopt when undertaking vulnerability testing. A main consideration is to conduct continuous scanning and point-in-time assessments in consideration of received vulnerability, exploit and threat information. From this, organisations should conduct a gap analysis from the results and apply secure configuration and patch management.

Another type of testing sometimes conflated with penetration testing is 'Red Team Assessment'. This involves an element of physical or electronic social engineering, and therefore end-user engagement in the testing process. It incorporates the practice of manipulating humans, rather than systems, to gain access to systems, and to test detection and response.

In effect, Red Team Testers run short cons (deceptions) against employees to determine and measure awareness and human vulnerabilities. With a phone call, phishing email or even a personal site visit, Red Testers will attempt to convince staff or others to reveal passwords, download code or unwittingly grant access to an unauthorised user in other ways, often over many weeks. Red Tests are not intended to be comprehensive, but rather to find a way to achieve the tester's goals. Much like penetration testing, Red Team Testing is determined by scope and can test multiple threat scenarios or very specific localised areas. In many instances, Red Teams are provided very specific areas of an organisation to focus on and exploit areas of weakness. The objectives are normally set from outputs of the Security Operations Centre (SOC) and include a multi-layered attack simulation to test human, network, applications and physical security. Similar to penetration testing, this is mostly carried out by external professionals, with only large organisations able to retain in-house services. Needless to say, the skill and complexity required to carry out this type of security function is by and large un-scalable.

One Red Tester metaphorically compared penetration testing versus Red Testing to pirates versus ninjas: pirates (penetration testers) are strong, execute brute force attacks and are good at plundering and long-range combat. However, pirates are loud, can be slapdash, and highly visible.

Ninjas (Red Testers), in contrast, are fleet, stealthy and dedicated to training and hand-to-hand combat. However, ninjas have no armour and are slight of size (Hayes, 2016).

Red Team Testers try to penetrate with stealth – testing the organisation's security processes and procedures. Whereas penetration testers are not trying to hide their objectives. Red Testing is suited to large organisations with sophisticated, mature systems and a broad security programme.

Establishing buy-in

Penetration tests are an excellent method of determining the strengths and weaknesses of a network of computers and network devices. Such testing serves many valuable purposes – these include:

- Identifying vulnerabilities that may be difficult or impossible to detect with automated network or application vulnerability scanning software.

- Assessing the magnitude of potential business and operational impacts of successful attacks.

- Meeting compliance standards which require regular penetration tests to ensure system security. For example, the Payment Card Industry Data Security Standard (PCI DSS[7]) requires annual penetration testing, and ongoing testing after any system changes.
- Penetration testing is essential as part of the change management process in critical web application development or IT infrastructure changes to ensure no new vulnerabilities have been introduced into the system by the changes.

It is important to align penetration test outcomes with realistic and reasonable requirements and expectations, as part of an overall technical security programme. This requires a risk management approach which considers, for example, the potential impact of a serious hacking incident resulting in a major data breach, variations in the general threat, or major alterations to business or systems processes, all of which could result in a potential loss.

As a component of a strategic view of security management, penetration testing can deliver many different and desirable benefits. The necessity and extent of the testing to be conducted should be based on the drivers and the criteria behind them, which are multiple. They may include compliance demands, awareness of actual attacks (successful or otherwise) on similar organisations; the impact of such attacks; significant changes to IT systems or operational processes; or a contractual obligation. Risk appetite is another factor to consider for reasons previously mentioned in this chapter. Typically, a combination of these factors drives penetration testing.

Senior management buy-in is essential, which means the language of penetration testing proposals and reports should provide context as well as technical review. They should avoid the extensive use of technical jargon which may not be understood by others within the organisation, and define such language when it is essential (even a phrase such as 'attack surface' is meaningless to most non-specialists without explanation), both at the outset and through to the reporting stage. This approach will help senior management and boards of directors to better understand the need for and benefits of testing. Budgets in most organisations are typically limited and mid-level managers can find it hard to get the necessary budget allocated, so using plain English is vital when making the case for penetration testing.

At this early stage, a test programme proposal should be prepared. It will set out the purpose of the activity, and outline potential benefits to the organisation, including the obvious (such as meeting a regulatory requirement) and the less tangible (for example, helping to avoid the reputational damage that can be incurred following a major security breach). In some cases, regular penetration testing in the past may be cited as a reasonable precaution to limit liabilities during a legal challenge.

The test programme proposal should also consider any potential limitations or pitfalls of testing.

Penetration tests have limitations, of course. For example, penetration testers must operate under certain constraints – such as time – which a real hacker would not necessarily face. Nor is a real hacker limited by any scope of testing. It is important to be aware of such limitations, and to design penetration tests accordingly.

DELIVERING MAXIMUM VALUE FROM PENETRATION TESTING

When considering penetration testing it is important to establish what exactly it is that needs to be achieved. Delivering maximum value from conducting penetration testing will depend entirely on the testers setting out a clearly defined statement of works and delivering within that. While there can be shortcomings in terms of not setting a clear scope and the very fact that systems frequently change, testers with the right tools and end-user engagement can expose critical business vulnerabilities and advise on delivering remediation – and this should always be at the forefront of the receiving organisation's mind.

Scope of testing

The scope of testing should be determined based both on the goals of the test and on the budget. To be effective, however, penetration testing requires an adequate budget and should not be minimised due to budgetary restriction, as half-measure penetration testing is a pointless exercise.

It is the job of the test programme proposal to justify and secure adequate funding for the scope of testing necessary. The scope may include the preferred profile of the threat agent, which could range from an external hacker with limited skills and no knowledge of the target system, to an internal user attempting to gain access to ring-fenced areas of the organisation's network. When the PCI DSS is to be applied for example (PCI Security Standards Council, 2015), all the 'people, processes, and technology that store, process, or transmit cardholder data or sensitive authentication data' are considered to form the 'cardholder data environment'. The standard requires penetration testing of public-facing potential entry points, as well as potential access points from within the system.

The terms black-box, grey-box and white-box are sometimes applied to penetration testing. The first implies the tester has no knowledge of the system, the third that full knowledge is provided in advance. Grey-box is often preferable, as it provides some internal knowledge of the network, such as a demonstration of the application being tested, and access to login credentials or internal architectural diagrams. This can reduce testing time without providing testers with too many keys to access before testing is under way.

Scope also defines the networks and systems to be tested. It may be that only public-access systems are to be tested, for example. Regardless of the approach, the challenge of defending the network perimeter is key to any testing. Firewalls should be installed and configured correctly at the time of testing. Penetration testing is one way to ensure this frontline defence is adequate.

At the outset, the client and tester should agree the scope and type or types of attack that will be implemented, and set clearly defined objectives. For example, it should be decided whether to adopt a white-, grey- or black-box attack approach, based on the business, sectoral and architectural risk analysis that preceded the process. Questions such as the range of IP addresses that will be swept and 'ping' tested should be agreed (the decision about the advanced supply of IP addresses to the tester is one to be made in the scope-setting process). Service Level Agreements (SLAs) should specify from the client any explicit permission to exploit any vulnerability as it is rare to have approval to exploit these at will. It would be prudent at the on-boarding, due-diligence stage to check with the vendor that they are insured to be able to provide such services. Penetration testing firms should have technology professional indemnity and cyber liability coverages.

Less technical variables should also be considered and agreed. For example, the client should ensure the price quoted is in line with overlying agreements. If the test service provider states its test will take five days, the limitations of testing within those five days should be defined. Once the objectives and scope of a given test are agreed, the client and the testing organisation should agree on the methodology to determine, after the fact, if the test objectives have been achieved.

Statement of works

Once a scope has been agreed, a clear statement of works should be provided, and a legal authorisation of those works provided in return. The latter should clearly state that the penetration testing organisation engaged can, in essence, 'attack' the contracting organisation without repercussions.

Timescales and delivery deadlines should be included in the statement of works. These variables will be dependent upon the type of attack required, the external and/or internal infrastructure to be tested, and the level of systems information the company wishes to provide before testing commences (all of which should be identified by the scope). When a penetration tester is given more information to reduce the level of reconnaissance required, testing will require less time. However, tests conducted by highly briefed testers do not provide a true reflection of the approach which might be adopted by a sophisticated threat agent.

Addressing potential shortcomings

Penetration testing has some shortcomings. One concerns timing. Any system can be tested at only one point in time and systems always change and evolve. So setting up a regular programme of testing with the appropriate time frequency is a prudent approach. Another shortcoming is scope. If satisfactory evaluation and planning are not carried out, the process can become a box-ticking exercise for the sake of compliance. It must be aligned to business goals and threats. The business, sectoral threats in the context of business risk analysis, and architectural risk analysis that precedes penetration testing will provide a useful map of priorities for the eventual penetration tests themselves. Understanding the threat by sector is critically important, as this analysis can help to determine the appropriate scope of testing. The same is applied when threat modelling against architectural considerations as this will help identify attack surfaces.

Testing on live systems carries risk, and the organisation should truly understand that risk before engaging in live testing. Often testing is carried out in non-work hours, which does not necessarily reflect the true operational environment (because, for example, many network devices may be switched off and un-ethical hackers work internationally and maintain unsociable hours).

At any time, penetration testing critical operating technology can be expensive and dangerous. There can be instances where aggressive vulnerability scans can cause network components to crash. If the limitations of tests are not well understood, it can in itself provide a false sense of security, especially in contrast to simple vulnerability scanning. No system is ever completely secure. However, penetration testing can help to build very high levels of confidence in the security of a system and the data it holds. To underpin this confidence, testing must not be a one-off process. When budgeting, a follow-up test should usually be factored in, since effective testing includes fixes: test, adjust and remediate, test again, then report.

Selecting the right tools

It is essential to ensure that penetration test outputs are accessible to existing cyber-security tools and programmes. The use of a risk tracking or vulnerability management tool assists in this by continuously detecting for common vulnerability exploits. Larger companies may have tracking remediation tools that follow developers' progress as bugs are repaired. Many organisations, particularly in the public sector, add vulnerabilities found in penetration testing to the organisation Risk Treatment Plan (sometimes called Risk Register). They may use these tools to grade the criticality of various security threats to prioritise remedial action. For example, a critical vulnerability that could expose large databases via the internet may require immediate mitigation, while similar data sitting on old unsuitable operating systems that run in isolation and do not connect directly to the corporate network may be a lower priority (although the potential vulnerabilities of such data warehouses should not be ignored).

In environments where software applications are built and managed internally, remediation tools should fit within a developers' software development lifecycle (SDLC). Ideally, a secure development programme will have been adopted early in the SDLC to prevent rather than identify vulnerabilities, although development should include penetration testing. At the post-implementation penetration testing stage, project management within a formalised process is necessary to ensure the capture of data and the validation of results and outputs throughout the lifecycle of the project. For the majority of organisations, however, third-party software applications are the norm for many functions and will carry an element of risk.

In security, an organisation is only as secure as its weakest link and third-party security assessments, dependent on criticality of the software asset, is essential. However, a major factor for consideration when reviewing a software provider is to assess the terms and conditions for guarantees that they penetration test their application. It is highly likely that they are providing the same service to other clients and will likely need to provide assurances that they are not introducing risk to their clients. As such, a software-as-a-service (SaaS) vendor will require clearly defined separate and limited rules of engagement for any of their customers who wish, in the course of due-diligence, to conduct a penetration test. Without this, the testing company risks being liable to potential prosecution.

End-user engagement with testing

As stated earlier in this chapter, for the majority of organisations penetration tests will be conducted with the assistance of a third-party penetration testing provider, although there will be certain organisations that will retain internal qualified testers – such as the UK Ministry of Defence (2013: 76) and large financial institutions. However, for those using third parties, in many cases, it may be appropriate to include administrator and end-user engagement with security testing programmes. If conducting a grey-box test for example, it is likely that the tester will require network or systems information from internal users – such as developers and other IT members.

Red Team Assessments, also discussed earlier, do involve end-users. They may unknowingly become involved, as Red Team testing involves the human side of breaching security, typically through physical and electronic social engineering.

In most cases, sensitive information will be shared with end-users only when testing has been truly disruptive to the business and demands immediate remedial attention. This and other reporting conditions and lines, particularly with senior management, should be agreed between testers and clients at the outset. A clear reporting line to senior management is an essential channel particularly for use when a critical threat to the business is uncovered.

Quality assurance

The role of a penetration tester is to determine what an intruder is able to do to gain access to a system or network and maintain access to that system or network, and what they could do with any information they find there. They do this with persistence and the deployment of learned skills to exploit weaknesses in targeted systems. Penetration testers should demonstrate to their clients any problems which they encounter or have uncovered. In some instances, the client will be unable to interpret the implementation instructions set out in the penetration tester's report. In such cases it is important that the tester is able to add clarity through illustration – for example, by delivering information to replicate the exploit to infiltrate a vulnerable part of the system and how to fix it via patches and code changes, among others. This is an important component of the validation process, because it delivers to clients the information necessary to understand vulnerabilities completely, and the processes employed by testers to exploit them.

When highlighting vulnerabilities, the importance of validation is underlined through its ability to identify false positives. Such wayward results can leave the client attempting to implement remedial actions to repair bugs and vulnerabilities that do not in fact exist. Validation should dramatically reduce the chance of this frustration occurring. It is part of a quality assurance process which should include the implementation of an auditing and tracking procedure.

Quality assurance on the part of the penetration test service provider is very important and must extend well beyond the actual outcome of the testing itself. Contracts can be lost for simple mistakes such as spelling errors in reports. In all cases, senior personnel (such as, in the UK, a qualified CHECK Team Leader) should at the very least review all penetration tests at all stages of the process. A UK-qualified CHECK Team Leader senior penetration tester will possess the background, experience and knowledge to assure the quality of the penetration testing work of junior testers. According to the UK National Cyber Security Centre (NCSC), a CHECK team is composed of at least one CHECK Team Leader and a number of CHECK Team Members who have passed any of the NCSC accredited CREST, Cyber Scheme, or Tigerscheme examinations. Only the NCSC may confer CHECK Team Leader/Member status.[8]

Review

Test review cycles should be set in consideration of the types of test to be deployed. One-off annual penetration tests for compliance are a norm, but penetration testing should also be conducted following major system changes or projects, as a component of security best practice, and as part of a holistic information security regime. Some large or extremely systems-dependent organisations opt for continuous testing, but this can be a significant consumer of management, staff and physical resources, potentially requiring weekly meetings and ongoing report reviews. It is common for large organisations to run regular monthly or weekly vulnerability scans and then engage with penetration testing teams annually or when major changes occur. For most medium to large organisations, a kick-off meeting or series of meetings before the test will be followed by daily wash-ups to highlight any considerations or requirements from either the testing team or organisation being tested, which may be handled as conference calls.

A penultimate meeting will consider important concluding questions, such as whether the overall aims and objectives of testing were achieved (and if not, why not), and should determine what next steps should be taken to meet the scope objectives. Another purpose of the meeting is to discuss a summary of the vulnerabilities uncovered, and to identify any critical databases which may be externally facing. A final wash-up should review and discuss an interim report that provides a summary of the entire testing process, its methodologies and its findings.

Recommendations for remediation

When the testing has been completed, the recommendations for remediation set by the tester should act as, or be interpreted much like any work instruction. In some instances, the IT manager or IT security manager will need to link the tester directly with the internal responder (for example, a developer), because internal personnel may not be able to rectify the issues identified, or may need further information to do so. It is not uncommon for the penetration tester to work alongside the appropriate personnel within the client firm's IT department to ensure these messages are delivered.

Benchmarking

Any firm that has engaged in a penetration testing programme should apply some basic benchmarking both of the penetration testers and the developers who will implement the remedies. At the most practical level, this could involve a simple assessment of the value-for-money of the penetration testing programme adopted. That said, there are many organisations who simply run a programme to satisfy governance requirements. Clients should consider the clarity of remediation recommendations made by their testers, and assess the speed of implementation of such remedies. If developers' coding practices are revealed to be sub-standard, more dialogue will be needed, perhaps alongside the introduction of structured methodologies to enable them to learn from their errors. Companies may seek to assess their security performance against an internal score card, or an international standard such as the Common Vulnerability Scoring System (CVSS), which provides a methodology to capture the main characteristics of a vulnerability and translate that vulnerability into a numerical score to reflect its severity. It allows informed allocation of resources to implement remediation. CVSS is a published, free international standard.[9]

PENETRATION TESTING AS PART OF A HOLISTIC INFORMATION SECURITY PROGRAMME

Penetration testing is a key part of a holistic information security programme. It should be considered as part of the overall security testing programme and its goals. As such, the frequency and depth of penetration testing should be aligned with other development and cyber-security projects. Some internet-based systems are tested annually. Other tasks demand project-based tests, such as code development and firewall configuration. A project test schedule is also needed when a heightened need for security is identified. For example, after a high-impact incident such as a malware or social engineering attack, an organisation is at a weak point. Once forensics have confirmed which part of an organisation has been exposed, it is highly likely that there will be IT-specific project streams working to reduce the likelihood of a repeat event. During this phase the organisation will be at a heightened level of security and might engage in penetration testing to measure the effectiveness of any change programmes. It could be that an organisation hasn't suffered an incident but has received a threat or near miss event. This could trigger the need to conduct project-based testing. Project-based testing may adopt one of many approaches, including wireless, application and comprehensive infrastructure testing.

One of the easiest ways to gain access to a network is through its wireless networks, so it is very important that Wi-Fi networks are segregated for internal private and guest Wi-Fi. It is important to make sure wireless configurations are as secure as possible. Using high-powered antennas and tools (such as the WiFi Pineapple,[10] a wireless penetration testing tool that acts like a 'man-in-the middle attack') hackers can attract users to log on through their access point, and then use software to track and log what connecting users do through its receiver. Segregation and strong encryption help minimise risk.

A man-in-the-middle attack is a form of interception attack. It is where someone has gained unauthorised access to communications between two parties for the purposes of eavesdropping or impersonation.

If conducting an infrastructure (network) attack it should form part of the penetration testing scope, as it is an easy route in for an attacker if there is no separation.

RISK ASSESSMENTS AND RELEVANCE TO LIVE-SYSTEM LIFECYCLES

Certain steps need to be taken before starting a penetration test to identify critical platforms and applications and also the internal IT personnel who will be part of the process. There are inherent risks that need to be properly assessed and where necessary, redundancies in place to manage and mitigate these.

Risk analysis and assessment

A risk analysis and assessment is critical before engaging in penetration testing. This is conducted in part to determine live systems' roles in enterprise IT. A first step is to identify, understand and map what data is held and how that data is classified. Critical platforms and applications can be identified through this process. A confidentiality, integrity, availability (CIA) assessment should form part of this process in order to determine the impact of a CIA breach:

- 'Confidentiality' is the rule-set that limits access to information held on systems to those authorised to see that information.

- 'Integrity' is the trustworthiness of that information – assurance it has not been tampered with at the stage of processing, transit or storage.

- 'Availability' is a promise of reliable access by those entitled to view and use the data.

Further, regulatory considerations may be at play, such as the aforementioned PCI DSS. All these factors should be included in the risk assessment process.

Live-system lifecycles

Live-systems personnel should be included in the process of penetration testing. Throughout the planning and testing periods, liaison with specified IT personnel responsible for live systems is an important link. The personnel who understand the environment best should always be on hand for consultation. If, for example, networks are undergoing penetration testing, the service manager of a data centre (DC) may need to be involved. Dependent on the size of the organisation and if cyber-attack response is part of the scope of the test, the individuals running the Network Operation Centre (NOC) and the Security Operation Centre (SOC) must be informed well in advance of any port scanning. In addition, developer or application support personnel should be on hand. Change management procedures must be followed closely, communication channels must be clear and people available and ready to provide assistance when needed. Another factor to consider is access to the DC. For some tests, it is a requirement to perform them at the DC and for many organisations, the DC is not run by them. Gaining the relevant access needs to be identified in the scope and clearly managed to avoid delays. Considerations can include but are not limited to the location of the DC and what tier of security the DC is – the higher the tier, the more security it will have in place.

System lifecycles and workloads should be considered in cyber-security threat schedules. This too should be considered in the risk assessment process, as it is important to understand where organisational vulnerabilities may lie. The global NotPetya attack during summer 2017 provided an excellent example of a system lifecycle threat. The malicious code used an auto-run function within a critical software update. It sought to gain administrator access, then to leverage that access across victim companies' entire networks. The potential impact of such attacks increases when companies 'whitelist' software updates, thus affecting live systems. Logic Bomb threats – malware timed to deploy at the time of an attacker's choosing – are another way to hack systems in alignment with system lifecycles.

System lifecycles may drive penetration testing schedules and scope when upgrades or maintenance operations are performed. PCI DSS requirements state that penetration tests must be performed at least annually to ensure that the controls assumed to be in place are still functioning effectively after any significant change to any part of the network infrastructure, after any application and software upgrade or maintenance, and immediately after a significant event. However, what is deemed significant is dependent upon the organisation's risk appetite and assessment. When a change could impact the security of the network or allow access to cardholder data, for example, it may be considered significant by the organisation in question.

SUMMARY

With an ever-increasing connectedness between people and systems, the need for organisations to penetration test those systems is expanding not only in scope but also in frequency. It is important to understand what you are trying to achieve when conducting a penetration test and the differences between this and vulnerability scanning.

When considering the services of a penetration testing company, understanding their background, qualifications and the frameworks they align to should be part of the procurement cycle. Whether conducted by internal or external resources, penetration testing should be realistic, have reasonable requirements and give support to the overall technical security programme. In all instances, it must be a risk-based, cost-effective approach to ensure money, time and resources are not wasted and objectives are achieved in line with the clear statement of works set out.

Before setting out on conducting a penetration test, organisations need to ask themselves, 'who is a threat to me and why?' and 'what does cyber risk mean to me?'. These two questions help identify the foundations for risk management – and the where and how of penetration testing might be applied.

REFERENCES

CREST (2017) *Penetration Testing Programme: Maturity Assessment Tools*. Available at: www.crest-approved.org/wp-content/uploads/Penetration-Testing-MMAT-Guide-2017. pdf

Hayes, K. (2016) Penetration test vs. red team assessment: The age-old debate of pirates vs. ninjas continues. *Rapid 7 Community*, 23 June 2016. Available at: https://community.rapid7.com/community/infosec/blog/2016/06/23/penetration-testing-vs-red-teaming-the-age-old-debate-of-pirates-vs-ninja-continues.

Ministry of Defence (2013) *Reserves in the Future Force 2020: Valuable and Valued.* Available at: https://assets.publishing.service.gov.uk/government/uploads/system/uploads/attachment_data/file/210470/Cm8655-web_FINAL.pdf

PCI Security Standards Council (2015) *Information Supplement: Penetration Testing Guidance.* Available at: https://www.pcisecuritystandards.org/documents/Penetration_Testing_Guidance_March_2015.pdf

3 REGULATORY MANAGEMENT FOR PENETRATION TESTING

Rob Ellis

We begin this chapter with an overview of regulation and compliance frameworks and how penetration testing fits in to them. The next section establishes the regulatory management approaches and considerations as well as the legal aspects that apply to conducting penetration testing. The final part of the chapter describes the main types of organisational regulation and compliance that apply to penetration testing.

GOVERNANCE AND REGULATORY COMPLIANCE OVERVIEW

Increasingly, high-profile security breaches have been in our headlines. For example, the 2013 breach of cardholder data at the US company Target led to costs to the company of US$252 million (McGinty, 2015). Arguably high-profile cases like this impact consumer confidence in online shopping (NCC Group, 2016).

Breaches like this cause direct and indirect damage to organisations themselves and to other organisations that they have a business relationship with or a responsibility for. Consequently, organisations have responded by employing a range of cyber-security technologies, policies, procedures and controls. At the same time, governments, regulatory bodies and industries have sought to improve and assure by responding with new and revised laws, regulations and compliance schemes aimed at preventing and mitigating such incidents. For example, following the 2017 Equifax breach, the US New York State Department of Financial Services announced that credit reporting agencies will now be required to register and comply with state cyber-security regulations (Clark, 2018).

With the scale and complexity of the systems used to deliver today's highly capable services, comes an increasing number of potential vulnerabilities lying in wait for discovery and exploitation. Penetration testing as a tool is used to discover the presence and extent of such vulnerabilities so that they can be assessed and resolved or mitigated before they can be exploited. On this basis, governments, regulatory bodies and businesses want to ensure that the organisations they work with are employing penetration testing effectively as one of the steps towards their information assurance.

Legal and regulatory requirements are by nature mandatory in that they apply to all. The EU General Data Protection Regulation (GDPR) as tailored by the UK Data Protection Act for example, applies to all processing of personal data of individuals (EU data subjects). Compliance frameworks are largely optional; however they can prove to be mandatory in practice when they are a requirement for access to an essential service that an organisation cannot operate without. This would include instances where a licence to operate will not be granted or will be withdrawn if an organisation is not compliant. The payment card industry's PCI DSS standard would be an example of this as organisations are required to demonstrate compliance to be permitted to process card payments.

Compliance frameworks such as the ISO27001:2013 information security standard are also available as a means for organisations to demonstrate that they operate to a specific standard. Demonstrating and certifying compliance with these standards can then be used competitively to differentiate from competitors as part of a strategy to generate new business or to protect existing business.

Key terms

When dealing with regulatory, legal and compliance frameworks, there are a number of applicable key terms and definitions. Key examples of these are described below.

Information governance
The organisational approach taken to meet regulatory, legal and risk requirements delivered through a system of policies, procedures and controls. Penetration testing in this context would be employed as part of an organisation's vulnerability management processes to treat risks presented by exploitable vulnerabilities. It would also typically be present in many of the regulatory and compliance standards that the organisation is required to meet.

Information assurance
The ability to provide confidence in the capabilities of an organisation's information systems to protect information. Penetration testing plays a key part in establishing this confidence by actively seeking to identify the presence of exploitable vulnerabilities so that they can be subsequently assessed and remediated or mitigated.

Regulatory bodies
Government or industry bodies charged with ensuring that organisations are operating in an appropriate manner. These organisations vary widely depending on the sectors that they are responsible for, but aspects of information security are a common theme among many of the regulations issued by them.

Compliance standards
Compliance standards are the framework of requirements set out by government, regulatory bodies and other organisations. These are set up to provide organisations with a specific baseline set of requirements they are to meet in order to demonstrate compliance.

Regulatory and compliance requirements
Regulatory requirements are the criteria that organisations are obliged to meet in order to operate legally; compliance requirements are those needed to achieve a compliant status.

Legal regulatory requirements would include national laws such as the UK Data Protection Act 2018/GDPR, Computer Misuse Act 1990 and Freedom of Information Act 2000. International laws could also apply such as the US Sarbanes–Oxley and Health Insurance Portability and Accountability Act (HIPAA) regulations.

Compliance frameworks and standards would vary based on organisation type, sector and organisational aims but could include ISO27001, PCI DSS and many others. These would frequently include an element of penetration testing specifically or indirectly as part of a wider requirement to manage risks from vulnerability exploitation.

REGULATORY AND LEGAL PREPARATORY CONSIDERATIONS

In preparing for penetration testing, an organisation needs to establish the overall requirements for a test, as shown in Figure 3.1. These will be based upon the organisation's legal, regulatory, compliance and information assurance requirements which will help to define which services are to be tested and how. These would be added to the penetration testing requirements from other areas such as responses to risks identified by the organisation's risk management processes or as preventive responses following security incidents.

Figure 3.1 Legal and regulatory requirements overview

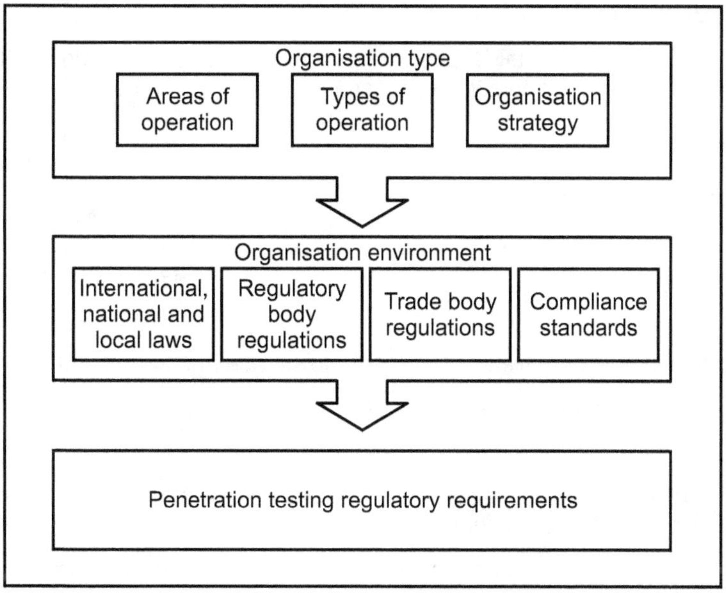

The legal requirements would be based upon the areas of operation and the subsequent local, national and international laws that apply to the organisation. The regulatory requirements would come from the type and activities of the organisation concerned.

Lastly, the compliance and standards requirements would be based on the standards that the organisation is maintaining or any that the organisation is seeking to meet as part of an organisational or business strategy.

In all cases, the requirements should factor in the laws, regulations and standards as they currently stand along with forthcoming changes. Researching such changes so that preparations can be made before they come into effect can be advantageous by helping to simplify introduction and minimise impact.

For services that are internal (services that are owned, managed and delivered by the organisation's resources) the penetration process will go through the organisation's processes to engage with the service owners. These processes would be specific to each organisation but could include elements from frameworks such as ITIL to ensure that testing is carried out on a formally agreed basis.

For contracted services that involve partners, suppliers (managed services or public cloud services for example) or other third parties, contracts will need to be reviewed to identify the basis for the penetration testing as follows:

- Is the penetration testing of the third party's service and its supporting infrastructure specified in the contract?
- Are there any contractual terms and conditions specifying how the penetration testing can be undertaken?
- Does the third party conduct its own penetration testing to a suitable level that will negate the need for further penetration testing?
- If there are contractual issues with carrying out the penetration testing, can the contract be updated to address these?

Public cloud services

Organisations subscribing to public cloud services will be required to enter a contractual relationship with the cloud provider. The terms and conditions for these services will typically include:

- The types of penetration testing of the service that are permitted.[1]
- The penetration testing actions that are allowed or prohibited.
- The notification that needs to be provided.
- Confidentiality and reporting of any cloud service vulnerabilities discovered by the penetration testing.
- The penetration testing and assurances given by the cloud provider.

Penetration testing contracts

Penetration testing may be carried out on behalf of the organisation by an external service provider or by an internal resource. Where the testing is to be carried out by an external service provider, a contractual relationship will be needed to establish the legal basis for the testing. Penetration testing may also be carried out in a hybrid manner using internal resources in conjunction with an external provider, in which case the considerations for both scenarios will apply.

Typically, the client organisation's contract with the service provider protects them as follows:

- Ensures that testing will only be carried out against services defined as being in-scope.
- Specifies how the testing will be conducted in terms of timing, locations and communications.
- Ensures ownership and confidentiality of the penetration testing results.
- Ensures retention and destruction of client data acquired during the testing.

The contract protects the penetration testing service provider as follows:

- Establishes that the client organisation is providing the permission for the testing against only their own services or their supplier-hosted services, granting the penetration test provider the legal authority to conduct the testing.
- Defines the overall scope of the testing to be carried out.
- Establishes the basis for the service provider's indemnity should the penetration testing disrupt services and cause subsequent damages.

Penetration test service provider accreditation

While in some instances there may not be a requirement for penetration test service providers to be accredited, organisations procuring penetration testing services may require assurance based upon industry accreditation.

The industry's main penetration testing accreditation is provided by the international not-for-profit accreditation body CREST.[2] Penetration testing providers can become members and be accredited in a number of information security disciplines including penetration testing. The application process assesses many factors including:

- quality procedures, policies and processes;
- penetration testing methodology;
- vetting and clearance of penetration testing personnel;
- qualifications and experience of penetration testing personnel;
- professional indemnity insurance level.

In addition to CREST, the UK's National Cyber Security Centre (NCSC) provides a similar accreditation known as CHECK[3] for penetration testing of UK government and critical national infrastructure systems.

Individuals can also become accredited through the Tigerscheme[4] and the Cyber Scheme[5] certifications. These schemes provide formal recognition to individuals and a number of the qualifications are recognised by the NCSC as part of CHECK accreditation.

In-house penetration testing

Where penetration tests will be carried out by an internal resource, the organisation needs to go through a process to develop a framework for the testing to be carried out in a controlled and approved manner. Without a supporting framework of policies and processes, the ability to carry out effective testing that meets requirements and identifies risks may be limited. In addition to this, employees engaged in penetration testing could find that their activities are not clearly authorised and could find themselves at risk of disciplinary action or prosecution.

To provide a framework for authorised penetration testing to take place by employees within an organisation, a penetration testing policy and process should be developed that specifies the following:

- roles and responsibilities;
- penetration testing authorisation and approval processes;
- training and organisation or employee accreditation;
- approved tools and methods;
- communication, notification and reporting;
- confidentiality and disclosure of the penetration test results;
- confidentiality, retention and destruction of any data acquired during the testing.

The findings of the penetration tests are critical and highly sensitive as they identify vulnerabilities within the organisation's systems; great care should be taken with the handling of this data. In addition to this, should the penetration testing directly or indirectly identify a breach that poses a risk to personal data, the relevant regulatory bodies must be notified. For the UK, the Information Commissioner's Office (ICO) must be notified unless the breach is unlikely to result in a risk to the rights and freedoms of individuals as defined under GDPR.

A review of other internal policies should be undertaken to ensure that they correctly reference and do not contradict the penetration testing policy. For example, acceptable use policies (AUPs) should define what unauthorised hacking is, while specifying that a penetration testing policy governs the permitted activities.

By establishing these policies and processes, employees can conduct the penetration testing in a legal and authorised manner.

Legal basis and authorisation

Whether the penetration testing is carried out by an external provider or by the organisation's in-house resources, there are laws that apply that will need to be followed to ensure testing is carried out on a legal basis. The applicable laws are as follows:

GDPR
Section 170 of the UK Data Protection Act 2018/GDPR refers to unlawfully obtaining personal data. If an employee engages in a penetration testing activity that results in

access to personal data without sufficient authorisation and without a legal basis, they could potentially face prosecution under this section of the act.

More on GDPR later in this chapter.

UK Computer Misuse Act (1990)

This Act[6] contains sections that could be presented if penetration testing activities are carried out without authorisation.

Section 1 of the Act refers to unauthorised access to computer material.

Section 3 concerns offences committed through unauthorised acts with intent to impair, or with recklessness as to impairing the operation of a computer. This could be presented if unauthorised penetration testing has disrupted services.

Section 3A concerns making, supplying or obtaining articles for use in offences under other sections of the act. This section of the act is primarily aimed at the illegitimate development and use of exploit tools such as malware. Penetration testing, however, also involves the development and use of tools designed to identify and exploit vulnerabilities – so authorisation for penetration testing is required to demonstrate that such use is legitimate and to avoid potential prosecution.

Section 3ZA applies to unauthorised acts causing or creating risk of serious damage. Again, as penetration testing has the potential to disrupt services, criminal offences could apply to penetration testing carried out without sufficient authorisation.

Organisations should put in place policies and notifications to specify to users that unauthorised access and activities contravene the Computer Misuse Act.

UK Health and Safety at Work etc. Act (1974)

This Act[7] contains a number of duties for employers and employees. These duties include ensuring the health, safety and welfare of employees and ensuring the public are not exposed to risks to their health and safety. There is also a duty requiring employees take care towards the health and safety of others that may be affected by their work activities.

Based on these duties, it is an offence under the act to fail to discharge them.

The nature of penetration testing will mean that there is a risk of disruption to the systems and services being tested. As penetration testing may cover production mission-critical systems it is essential to put in place measures to ensure health and safety as far as is reasonably practical. Failure to do so could result in criminal offences under this act, based on failing to discharge the duties.

Additional considerations

Whether the penetration testing is carried out by an external or an internal resource the governance and regulatory aspects related to employees need to be considered. Examples would include the handling of any personal data obtained during the testing in a manner that is compliant with data protection regulations and the organisation's policies.

Consideration should also be given to the regulatory and legal aspects of employee-owned devices used as part of an organisational bring-your-own-device (BYOD) service. Issues that should be considered include the accidental capture of data from such devices and handling of any risks identified on employee-owned devices during the testing. Policies and processes should be in place to govern BYOD and the inclusion of penetration testing aspects will help to ensure that there are no surprises.

An additional area that may be included as part of a penetration test programme is the use of social engineering to test the effectiveness of policies, processes and training. To ensure this is carried out on a legal basis, this should be defined, reviewed and authorised by an organisation. This should include:

- ensuring specific consent is in place for the social engineering attempts;
- ensuring that appropriate[8] communication has been carried out;
- ensuring individual employee rights are not compromised.

SECTORS AND COMPLIANCE STANDARDS

Like a jar of assorted buttons, the diverse range of laws, regulations, standards and compliance schemes related to penetration testing can be categorised based on many different criteria: International or national? Public or private sector? Mandatory or optional? Industry or functional area?

Some regulations will be legally based, applying horizontally to specific areas of a wide range of organisations such as financial functions. Others will be highly specific applying only to organisations operating within a specific vertical sector such as nuclear industries.

Horizontal sector examples

The remit of data protection regulations such as the EU General Data Protection Regulation (GDPR) cover the handling and protection of all personally identifiable data for all organisations within the EU or processing the data of EU citizens.

Financial accounting regulations such as the US Sarbanes–Oxley Act span the accountancy functions of all businesses with a listing in the United States. Section 404 of this Act applies to information security and penetration testing as it mandates the establishment of internal controls and procedures. It also requires the maintenance and testing of controls and procedures to ensure their effectiveness. Focused penetration testing and reporting can be carried out to specifically meet Sarbanes–Oxley compliance requirements.

Vertical sector examples

Nuclear regulation in the UK is carried out by the UK Office for Nuclear Regulation (ONR). Its regulatory responsibilities apply to the nuclear aspects of all civilian organisations, including:

- nuclear material transportation;
- nuclear energy generation;
- nuclear fuel processing;
- nuclear site decommissioning;
- emergency preparation and response.

The ONR regulates these areas on a compliance and guidance basis. The published guidance (ONR, 2017) for ONR's inspectors makes several references to penetration testing as a means for organisations to demonstrate their information assurance.

Other regulatory bodies or legislation may apply to specific sectors. For example, in the US, the Health Insurance Portability and Accountability Act (HIPAA) regulates the privacy and security of individually identifiable health information for US citizens. This legislation consequently applies to care providers, medical insurers, researchers, pharmaceutical companies and many others.

The high dependence of all organisations upon electronic information-based services means that most regulatory standards will have elements of information security. As a key means of securing any information-based service, the effective application of penetration testing will directly or indirectly feature in these.

Regulatory bodies and legislation

Regulatory bodies vary based upon the sector they are responsible for regulating. They may apply their regulatory powers through legal measures or on a basis of guidance and recommendations.

In the UK, the ICO with the protection of personal data as its remit is responsible for the enforcement of GDPR/Data Protection Act 2018. Because of the nature of personal data, these legal requirements cover the operations across most, if not all, sectors and industries.

General Data Protection Regulation (GDPR)/UK Data Protection Act 2018

GDPR is an EU regulation that, following a two-year adoption period, was implemented across the EU in 2018 with nation specific tailoring implemented in the UK in the form of the UK Data Protection Act 2018. The aim of the regulation is to strengthen and unify data protection across the EU. The UK Data Protection Act

2018 supplements GDPR into UK law with UK-specific provisions. GDPR applies to personal data and defines the obligations for organisations to protect such data in terms of Data Controllers, Data Processors and principles. Data Controllers are the organisations that, following consent, are collecting personal data from citizens. Data Processors are organisations that are processing personal data as a service on behalf of Data Controllers.

Article 5 of the GDPR states that personal data shall be 'processed in a manner that ensures appropriate security of the personal data, including protection against unauthorised or unlawful processing and against accidental loss, destruction or damage, using appropriate technical or organisational measures'.

This is followed by a requirement that 'the controller shall be responsible for, and be able to demonstrate, compliance with the principles'.

Article 32 of GDPR further specifies that measures to be implemented should include 'a process for regularly testing, assessing and evaluating the effectiveness of technical and organisational measures for ensuring the security of the processing'. Penetration testing in most circumstances will be considered as one of the most effective means of meeting this requirement. In addition, as a means of identifying potential vulnerabilities, it also presents a valuable means for organisations to demonstrate compliance with the principles based upon the effectiveness of other security measures.

The GDPR includes principles[9] for personal data such as the right to erasure – individuals can request that an organisation deletes their personal data. These principles should be considered in terms of any personal data obtained during the penetration testing.

In the event that a breach is discovered that affects (loss, alteration or destruction) personal data and there is a resultant risk to the rights and freedoms of individuals, GDPR establishes a requirement for notification.[10] This notification will be to the relevant supervisory authority (ICO) and directly to the individuals. Notifiable breaches must be reported within 72 hours and must be done without undue delay if the breach is sufficiently serious.

The adoption of GDPR in the UK alongside the 2018 Data Protection Act has resulted in a significant increase in the size of penalties that can be imposed for failures to protect personal data (€20 million or 4% of total annual worldwide turnover) and the increased requirements represent a greater compliance challenge for organisations to meet.

Trade body compliance

Compliance frameworks from trade bodies are typically established as a means of ensuring standards are met before trade services will be offered. These could range from highly specific standards set by individual companies to widely applicable standards such as the PCI DSS standard that organisations are required to meet for them to be able to process card payments. Many of these standards, like the PCI DSS, have evolved to include information security requirements including penetration testing.

Payment Card Industry Data Security Standard (PCI DSS)

The PCI DSS is an industry compliance standard established by the major card companies as a means of combating credit card fraud by increasing security controls. The degree of compliance validation varies according to the nature and scale of the card handling organisation. Small volume organisations can self-assess against the standard, while larger organisations will be assessed by an external qualified security assessor or an internal security assessor.

Since being established in 2004, PCI DSS has been repeatedly updated with additions being initially added as guidance before being changed to mandatory requirements as the version of the standard is updated. This approach gives organisations awareness and time to prepare for the changes. Penetration testing is one such area that has evolved significantly through the updates to the standard.

Requirement 11 of the standard now requires organisations to regularly test security systems and processes. Section 11.3 specifically requires organisations to establish a methodology for annual external and internal penetration testing. As key elements of the standard cover the segmentation of the cardholder data environment from other areas of the organisation's infrastructure, this testing must also be carried out after changes to the controls that provide this segmentation.

Non-governmental organisation (NGO) compliance frameworks

Many compliance standards are established by non-government organisations. Arguably, the most significant information technology and information security standards have been developed by the International Organization for Standardization (ISO). The most relevant standard to penetration testing is ISO's Information Security Standard ISO 27001:2013. This standard provides a specification of processes and policies for the establishment of an Information Security Management System (ISMS). This can be scoped to apply to the entire organisation or to specific organisational areas or functions that can choose to adapt their information security policies and procedures to make themselves compliant with the standard.

Organisations can then proceed to be independently assessed by an accredited party in order to certify their compliance. This certified compliance may then enable access to business contracts that require compliance and it also helps the organisation to differentiate themselves from competitors.

Section 12.6 of Annex A of the ISO 27001:2013 specifies an objective to reduce the risks resulting from the exploitation of published technical vulnerabilities. This has an associated control to obtain, assess and apply appropriate measures to meet the objective. An established penetration testing process provides an essential means of compliance with this requirement.

Types of compliance conformity

Aligned
Adaptation and alignment of an organisation's processes to be similar in practice or spirit to a framework.

Compliant
The organisation is compliant with a framework based on self-assessment or assessment by a third party.

Certified
The organisation or specific sections are verified and certified against a framework by an independent accredited body.

Accredited
Independent organisations that are accredited by the standards bodies to assess and certify other organisations.

There are a number of frameworks for governing enterprise information technology and ensuring alignment of IT with business objectives.

COBIT

COBIT is one such framework that defines a maturity model and specifies processes, controls and guidelines that, when implemented well, can contribute to achieving and maintaining regulatory compliance.[11] COBIT is a high-level framework and recent iterations have included updates to enable it to be aligned with more detailed frameworks such as the ITIL framework described next.

ITIL, ITSM, ISO20000

Alongside the ISO 27001:2013 Information Security standard, there are also standards for Information Technology Service Management (ITSM). The employment of these frameworks of IT processes can be used as a means of simplifying and demonstrating regulatory compliance. These frameworks can also assist with the development and integration of penetration testing as part of other IT processes.

For example, based upon the ITIL® ITSM framework,[12] an organisation can establish operational level agreements (OLAs) to describe the inter-group responsibilities, processes and schedules to support the delivery of the penetration testing service. For penetration testing services, these would include such things as information provision, notifications, approvals, communications and resourcing.

The penetration testing service owner can then define and agree a service level agreement (SLA) for the delivery of the service to the organisation. The SLA will include the penetration testing service definition, responsibilities and targets.

Lastly, ITSM certification can also be obtained through the ISO20000 ITSM compliance standard.

Business Continuity ISO 22301

ISO 22301 is the ISO's Business Continuity Management Standard. The adoption of this standard provides organisations with a means to respond in the event of disruption to services. While steps should be taken to minimise the risk of service disruption resulting from penetration testing, intrusive probing can have unforeseen consequences. Mature business continuity processes provide organisations with a degree of assurance that should any service-disrupting events occur, they can be responded to in a planned manner that minimises impact.

The development of business continuity processes may also provide the penetration testing teams with isolated test environments in which to conduct the testing without being held back by the fear of live service disruption. If this approach is used, care should be taken to ensure that penetration testing remains an effective assessment of what is in place in the organisation's production environments.

SUMMARY

In summary, regulations and compliance schemes are the measures that are used to establish a minimum standard of information governance, minimising risk to all parties. Many compliance schemes will specifically require penetration testing processes, and those that do not will typically require it by implication. This creates a need for organisations to manage how regulation and compliance fit into their penetration testing and how penetration testing fits in with their regulation and compliance.

REFERENCES

Clark, D.M. (2018) 'In wake of Equifax data breach, credit reporting agencies made subject to NY State cybersecurity regulations'. *New York Law Journal*, 25 June 2018. Available at: https://www.law.com/newyorklawjournal/2018/06/25/in-wake-of-equifax-data-breach-credit-reporting-agencies-made-subject-to-ny-state-cybersecurity-regulations/?slreturn=20190423063530

McGinty, K.M. (2015) Target data breach price tag: $252 million and counting. *Mintz*, 26 February 2015. Available at: https://www.mintz.com/insights-center/viewpoints/2826/2015-02-target-data-breach-price-tag-252-million-and-counting

NCC Group (2016) 63% of consumers think their financial information will be hacked within the next year. Available at: https://www.nccgroup.trust/uk/about-us/newsroom-and-events/press-releases/2016/january/63-of-consumers-think-their-financial-information-will-be-hacked-within-the-next-year/

Office for Nuclear Regulation (2017) *Protection of Nuclear Technology and Operations*. Available at: www.onr.org.uk/operational/tech_asst_guides/cns-tast-gd-7.3.pdf

4 EMBEDDING PENETRATION TESTING WITHIN ORGANISATIONAL SECURITY POLICIES AND PROCEDURES

Ceri Charlton

An important part of the strategy of utilising penetration tests is identifying when they are to be used. This chapter discusses the way in which the activities relating to penetration testing can be built into the Information Security Management System (ISMS) of an organisation and the broader risk management framework. This chapter aims to explore some of the drivers, approaches and obstacles to embedding penetration testing (however it may be conducted) within an organisation.

ADDING PENETRATION TESTING TO AN EXISTING ENTERPRISE INFORMATION SECURITY STRATEGY

Increasingly, regardless of any additional industry-specific or regulatory requirements, penetration testing is legally becoming an expectation: the legal view is moving towards a stance that penetration testing is not just a 'nice to have' or something that conscientious, 'best in class' organisations undertake. The absence of evidence of penetration testing having been performed is increasingly viewed as negligence.

As an example, the investigation conducted by the ICO in 2017 specifically cited the failure of Boomerang Video Ltd to conduct regular penetration testing on its website, as a factor in its determination that Boomerang took inadequate steps to protect the data that it held.[1]

In this case, Boomerang was a company which provided rentals of videogames to customers, in exchange for payment, made via an e-Commerce portal. The portal was originally developed almost a decade prior to the breach, but since then, had not been subjected to regular penetration testing. In investigating the breach, the ICO determined that: (i) customers' payment card information had been accessed by the attacker; and (ii) this had been possible due to vulnerabilities existing within this platform.

One of the particularly inexcusable vulnerabilities cited was SQL Injection, which existed within the login screen. Exploiting this flaw, the attacker was able to cause the web page to return details of both usernames and the hashes of the passwords associated with these accounts. At the time of the breach occurring, SQL Injection specifically had been a disclosed class of vulnerability for over a decade and a half and OWASP (the Open Web Application Security Project) had included input validation and injection vulnerabilities among its 'Top Ten' common vulnerabilities for around a decade. The existence of these vulnerabilities is trivially easy to test for and can even be discovered using automated tools. It is unlikely that vulnerabilities as obvious and easy to detect as this would have been overlooked during penetration tests performed by any competent tester.

It is interesting to note that even though the insecure portal was developed by a third party, Boomerang was found to be at fault for failing to detect the vulnerabilities, due to this lack of penetration testing.

Not all penetration tests are created equal and indeed, there is a great deal of variation in terms of how regularly organisations conduct penetration tests. In the Payment Card Industry, Data Security Standard (PCI DSS) and its related standards, we see that a failure to have performed a penetration test for a new system ahead of deployment to production is considered a compliance violation in itself, as is failure to re-test any system, at least once a year after the last test.

By building penetration testing into an organisation's ISMS, an organisation achieves several things:

- It is clearly presentable to any external parties reading formal security documentation, such as prospective customers, regulators or legislators, that there is an expectation that penetration testing is performed.

- It eliminates the excuse of individuals or projects within the organisation in the position to be able to deploy new software that they had not realised that it would be necessary.

- It formalises the expectation of penetration testing, which in turn allows internal or external auditors, who base the scope of their own assessment on the stated requirements of the organisations' governance, to validate that such testing has occurred.

- It may assist those procuring software to also secure the budget to have penetration testing performed.

PREPARATION AND PLANNING

When attempting to build penetration testing into existing security requirements and testing procedures, IT management should consider:

- **Which** systems require penetration testing? All? Those where the risk warrants it? Only where mandated by regulation?

- How **frequently** are tests and re-tests required? Is there a requirement to periodically re-test even unchanged legacy systems, in case newly disclosed vulnerabilities have emerged since the last test?

- How **significant** must a release be, before it requires a re-test? Is it only necessary for major releases, or after every patch? In order to meaningfully answer this question, it is also necessary to formally and explicitly state the means by which a release will be categorised. For example, does changing a specific number of screens or forms constitute a major release, or is anything larger than a 'bug fix', that is anything introducing new functionality, a release which necessitates a re-test?

- Is it acceptable to constrain the **scope** of the penetration test to only those elements or modules of an application that have changed?

- **Where** will penetration testing occur? Is the organisation highly security-oriented and is penetration testing in production justifiable in order to minimise threats introduced in deployment? Is the organisation's availability so critical that tests can only ever be sanctioned in pre-production environments?

- Can the organisation **afford** the desired rate and thoroughness of testing (costs consisting not only of that of the testing itself, but the subsequent remediation of findings and retesting, as may be necessary)? Do lower sensitivity systems really warrant the cost of a lengthy third-party test, relative to the risks they pose?

- What would be the **consequence** of a decision not to penetration test?

- What **commitments** have been made (or are likely to need to be made in the foreseeable future) regarding the performance of penetration testing? Do any customers have an expectation, or contractual permission to see the results? Do any regulatory standards which apply require penetration testing?

Once made, these decisions should be formally recorded, along with narrative justifying these choices. Doing so will not only make these choices more defensible in future, but it will also help drive good decision-making in the first instance. Furthermore, perhaps less obviously, it will assist when periodically reviewing these decisions in future. Specifically, if the historical reason for a given stance is formally recorded, it will be much more readily apparent if this reason no longer applies and hence the stance should be reconsidered.

As well as building these requirements into documents such as the Information Security Policy, consideration should be given to other existing documentation which ought to be updated to reflect the decided-upon strategy. For example, Software Development Life Cycle (SDLC) documentation needs to have its 'testing' section and diagrams updated to explain the location(s) in which penetration testing is expected to occur.

Even once formalised and captured in documentation, it should not be assumed that this will translate easily or quickly to these requirements being followed as a matter of course within the organisation. There should be an exercise of communicating this to all parties involved in the implementation of new systems. As well as the (perhaps obvious) candidates of technical IT staff, individuals in project management and programme management, there are also key stakeholders who need to understand these requirements. The attribution of responsibility for ensuring that penetration tests are undertaken needs to be formally defined and allocated to a specific party, or class of parties; otherwise there is a danger that it will be missed. One traditionally popular approach is to make the information security team responsible for performing the testing, or ensuring that the testing is performed.

Given the growing tendency for 'Shadow IT',[2] however, this increasingly includes individuals outside the IT department. Ideally, anyone in a position to purchase software or systems (i.e. any budget holder) would be aware of these requirements. Such responsibilities usually need to not only be communicated, but to be documented, in order to create the accountability that may otherwise be missing, without this clarity. As an example, less knowledgeable system owners, especially those outside the IT department, may incorrectly presume that IT, or information security, are automatically aware of the existence of **all** systems associated with the organisation and will facilitate penetration testing on their behalf. This also presumes that such parties will have some degree of understanding of what a penetration test is and that it is something necessary to perform: an assumption which is not always correct.

Should any changes be made to the organisation's stance on penetration testing, this should not only be re-communicated, but the appropriate documentation updated. An example of why this might occur would be changing regulatory requirements, or revised risk appetites following an information security incident within the organisation.

ALIGNMENT OF POLICIES AND PROCEDURES WITH THE CHANGING NATURE OF THREATS

IT is a fast-moving discipline in general and information security even more so. A key part of maturity with regards to a penetration testing strategy is recognition that the strategy itself should be reviewed regularly and, where appropriate, adjusted. Ideally, when a review of documentation which defines an approach to penetration testing is performed, it should not just be reviewed from the perspective of ensuring it reflects the current reality within the organisation. Rather, the appropriateness of the strategy itself should be considered and re-evaluated.

It is generally expected that those parties who are determining and reviewing the strategy remain up to date in their knowledge of threats and controls which are expected to mitigate them, and how the validation of the effectiveness of these controls can be built into the scope of penetration tests. Failure to do so will result in a strategy that quickly falls out of date: for example, by failing to consider fundamentally new threats such as changes in the way in which network connectivity is provided or how a user's identity is validated.

Following any information security incident which involved a breach of a system, it would be a sensible approach to review the strategy which determines when penetration testing is necessary. For example, by asking questions such as:

- Would a penetration test have detected the vulnerability which was used to gain access to the system?

- Would a penetration test have pre-emptively identified that the control that failed was not operational?

- Would a penetration test have identified that there was no control in place?

Updating the organisation's strategy (and associated policies and procedures) based on these answers means a more appropriate position on the use of penetration testing can be reached. Where obstacles to penetration testing (budget, prioritisation of new features over security fixes and so on) have previously been met, the tangible and close proximity of a security incident within an organisation can often have a sobering effect that subsequently removes these obstacles.

Another consideration in larger organisations is what other parts of the same group or corporation are doing and the services they offer. For example, one part of a software house might be producing marketing web pages, where a breach may have lower material impact; whereas another area of the organisation might make software for the financial services. The reputation of the latter will likely be harmed by association with a breach occurring in the former. This risk can mean that in some organisations it is prudent to adopt a 'blanket' requirement to penetration test **all** systems; even ones with a marginal degree of material risk.

Even in smaller organisations, the future strategy will play a part. Embedding penetration testing and developing maturity takes time. It can be a wise strategy to initiate it **before** it becomes a firm requirement for customers or regulatory drivers force it. This way, the inevitable teething problems can be overcome before the stakes are high enough that failing a penetration test and its re-test has a high consequence, or affects the decision to release a highly anticipated new version of a piece of software.

Budgetary and costing issues

No matter how efficient or leanly run, all forms of penetration testing are, in the short term, more expensive than not testing. At a high level a decision not to perform a penetration test can be seen as short-term gain (in terms of cheaper new software and system) at the cost of long-term risk.

When explaining to C-Level management, aside from providing the cost breakdown of the penetration tests themselves, it is important to highlight other factors that impact the cost to benefit to be considered. These include:

- **Scale of coverage.** A modest penetration testing budget can still achieve something meaningful when sensibly targeted at the most important system, or the one containing the most high-risk information, even if nothing else on the estate is tested.

- **Customer expectation.** Increasingly, customers are asking vendors for assurances that they perform penetration testing, before procuring their services. This is becoming increasingly true, even in markets such as retail, travel and hospitality, which have not historically been seen as security-conscious. This point can often be used to 'sell' some of the benefits of investing money in penetration testing, particularly if an organisation has encountered such questions from prospective customers.

- **Regulatory.** Generally, regulatory pressures are shifting to try to incentivise the desired behaviour of performing penetration testing; or, at least, to make the cost:benefit ratio of performing such tests appear more desirable. A particularly prominent example at present is GDPR, with fines of up to 4 per cent of group turnover for any organisation that has had a breach of personal data.

- **Brand preservation.** Commonly, people only consider the direct monetary loss of a breach, or any resultant fines when making a cost:benefit analysis of penetration testing. While this is somewhat understandable, given the good cost transparency that exists, it is far from the only cost. Notoriously difficult to calculate, brand damage and a loss of trust (and consequently, custom) are very real risks of a breach. What should be clearly communicated is that even when it is unsuccessful in preventing a breach, the performance of penetration testing has some benefit in reputational damage limitation. An organisation that took all reasonable steps and was hacked anyway is far more likely to be quickly forgiven than one which was deemed to be negligent and skimping on basic security controls such as penetration testing, which have now become an expectation.

After-effects of a breach

Earlier in this chapter, we discussed Boomerang Video Ltd. Even though the breach is over and, presumably, the vulnerabilities concerned have long since been addressed, it is still mentioned when the organisation's name comes up. Looking at discussions and reviews of the company online, it was still possible in 2018 to find both message-board discussions criticising handling of the breach and ratings site posts of the company, which reference the breach and which continue to directly impact contemporary ratings of the company. The ease of searching for reviews online means that many consumers' personal 'due-diligence' consists of researching a company in this way and critical comments such as these continue to influence those considering using the service. Although it is next to impossible to determine precisely how many potential new customers are still being lost, it is safe to say that senior management and the marketing department within the organisation would prefer not to have this persistent reputational damage.

There is some discussion by commentators that have performed analysis on the post-breach share price of organisations and surveyed the general perception of the (current) trustworthiness of a company after a breach, which suggest the effects do not last forever. It appears that the negative effect is most prominent immediately after the breach but over a period (estimates vary, but appear to be a year, possibly two), the organisation tends to return to the former position (author's generalisation of research findings).

Cost:benefit of penetration testing

Penetration testing, regardless of whether it is performed internally or externally, invariably requires resources to perform. In organisations that have not previously performed penetration testing, or have done so only sporadically, it is likely that doing it regularly will be perceived as a fundamentally new or additional cost by budget holders and, as such, may be met with resistance.

Some of the benefits that can be presented, which may help offset the negative perception of this cost are:

- less need to invest in marketing activities to offset reputational damage following a breach;

- lessening (or even total avoidance) of regulatory fines;

- increased market share due to increased faith in solution by customers, as testing occurs;

- avoidance of potential loss of customers following a breach;

- early detection of security defects mean they can be remediated sooner in the process, ultimately more cheaply.

Who will conduct penetration tests going forward?

In many cases, rather than defining who will **perform** the test, it makes sense instead to define who is responsible for **ensuring that the test is performed**. For example, an organisation may determine that the chief information security officer (CISO) is ultimately responsible for ensuring that a penetration test is performed, without expecting them to perform it themselves. Such a choice of stance also provides flexibility as to how tests are carried out. If there are other stakeholders who require penetration testing to be performed, these too are to be considered and expressly stated.

For example, an organisation may have a variety of systems and may make the strategic decision that only certain key systems warrant the additional assurance of a penetration test. At the same time, this may be governed by regulatory drivers for particular data, or for systems connected to related organisations with high security requirements (for example, banks directly connected to a financial institution).

Where this is the case, a statement of which systems must be tested and by whom may be appropriate. For example, appropriate text might read:

> The budget holder who funds the purchase and support of a given IT system is identified by default as the Owner of the system. Owners are responsible for determining whether they consider the risk posed by the data in a given system warrants the additional protection and assurance provided by a penetration test. [Company] recognises that for its systems which are directly connecting to the Government Connect Secure Extranet (GCSX) network, it is a requirement to utilise CREST- or CHECK-certified external penetration testers.

Where broader internal risk management frameworks exist, it can be useful to also introduce a requirement to formally capture (perhaps as a part of a project initiation document) the basis on which the decision whether to test or not was made. By insisting upon such a justification, it encourages consistency with the organisation's stated stance on when penetration tests are to be used. If there are genuine reasons why a penetration test is not necessary, it allows them to be captured, so that these are more readily apparent to any parties scrutinising this decision subsequently. Similarly, it is clear that there was a conscious decision **not** to test, rather than simply that an oversight to test is trying to be dishonestly justified after the fact. Such decisions must of course take into consideration the requirement of any applicable legislation, such as PCI DSS or the Health Insurance Portability and Accountability Act (HIPAA), which explicitly requires a penetration test to be performed.

AWARENESS RAISING AND NOTIFICATION

Dependent upon the scope and nature of the testing, there may be no need to notify the broader community; for example, a test solely designed as an application test, which seeks only to discover vulnerabilities in code and explicitly excludes vulnerabilities in infrastructure and platforms used to host the software. In such a test, it may be possible to provide testers with the code away from your production environment and no one outside the development team needs to be aware that it is being carried out.

As soon as the scope of the test touches **any** infrastructure which is shared with production systems, at a minimum, this question needs to be considered: Is there a significant enough chance of affecting production to warrant notifying users, or at least system owners?

Depending upon the answer to this question, decisions need to be made as part of the change management process as to who does need to be notified. For example, unless it has expressly been requested, penetration tests typically omit actually validating the existence of a suspected DoS (Denial of Service)[3] vulnerability, for fear of causing genuine disruption to live services. Therefore, depending upon the level of confidence that the test can be conducted in a manner that is highly unlikely to affect production systems, it may be decided to narrow the number of parties who are notified.

At the same time, even the most careful penetration tester may accidentally affect production systems. Some of the reasons for this include:

- poor scoping by the party commissioning the test;
- changes made to the environment during the window of time between the definition of the scope and the performance of the test;
- automated tools, particularly 'spidering' discovery tools, straying beyond the intended boundaries;
- omissions by the penetration tester of clauses that limit the range of a given test, or other syntactic errors of limit conditions;
- human operator error, for example, typing the wrong IP address of the system to test.

Given this potential for such mistakes, consideration needs to be given to the consequences of a mistake and what this could mean for the environment at large. As a general rule, in lieu of any other agreement, the level of seniority within an organisation, appropriate for providing 'sign-off' authorisation of the test needs to be at least as high as that of the ownership of the system being tested. A test of a small system used by only the human resources (HR) department could reasonably be sanctioned by the HR manager responsible for running it. Conversely, it could reasonably be argued that any test of the main production system be signed off by the COO (chief operations officer), or at least an individual the COO has explicitly empowered to do so on their behalf.

OTHER FACTORS FOR CONSIDERATION

Given the growing trend towards adopting cloud-based, or software as a service (SaaS), applications, consideration must be given to the need to adequately treat the risks of vulnerabilities, where penetration testing cannot necessarily be performed by the customer consuming the services. Unlike 'on-premise' solutions, SaaS frequently has services shared between multiple customers. Vendors sometimes argue (sometimes legitimately and sometimes from a position of cynicism and excuse-making) that they cannot permit a customer to perform a penetration test for fear that it will cause disruption to other customers, or even result in the disclosure of other customers' data.

One approach to deal with this increasingly popular model of software is to ensure that responsibilities for some equivalent form of testing being carried out are clearly allocated. The most common means of doing so are to either: (i) reserve the right to perform (or for a third party of the client's choice to perform) a test of the system; or (ii) require the organisation providing the solutions to offer evidence that they have arranged for this to be performed on the customers' behalf.

The general trend is towards organisations favouring option 2 (ii) for SaaS which is general, rather than a solution specifically produced for a single customer. Typically, this model requires that it is a suitably qualified, independent third-party penetration tester that performs the test. A legitimate reason for using a single third party is that it would be impractical to permit a thousand customers on a shared environment to each conduct their own penetration tests, according to their own schedules.

What remains contentious, however, is the level of detail of information which vendors are expected to share with customers regarding the tests. This is of course open to negotiation, between client and vendor, but factors which generally play a significant part in the outcome include the following:

- **Regulatory model governing the service** – Does the customer, or the customers' auditor, have an explicit need to see the results of the penetration test?

- **Customer's size, relative to that of the vendor** – An especially large or important customer may be able to convince a vendor to disclose a greater level of detail than a smaller one might. Similarly, blue-chip 'Mega Vendors' will often get away with citing that the sheer quantity of customers they have prevents them from deviating from a 'one size fits all' model, which they implement for all customers and effectively refuse to enter into negotiations with individual customers in this respect.

- **Level of security maturity of the vendor** – A vendor with a high degree of confidence both in their current security posture and their ability to remediate any future penetration test findings is likely to be more willing to be transparent with the results of tests than a vendor who is not.

Although far from standard or formalised, there are some generally emerging conventions with regards to which information specifically is shared. It is generally difficult for a vendor to argue against sharing:

- the fact that penetration testing occurs (or not) for a given system and the frequency with which this is performed;
- whether the testing is performed by a third party or internal resource;
- whether any certifications or accreditations are necessary for the testers to be eligible to perform tests (for example, CREST or CHECK certified);
- the scope of the test and, crucially, confirming that the system or service(s) under discussion are included within the scope of this test.

Again, negotiation is possible, but vendors tend to be more reluctant to formally agree to the following:

- The detailed results of previous tests, including the specific vulnerabilities and where in the system that they exist.
- To notify the client as soon as a vulnerability is discovered by any future penetration test.
- The time frames in which they will fix any vulnerabilities detected by a test and that they will provide evidence of this remediation by sharing details of the results of a re-test covering the specific vulnerabilities which have been discovered.

Another factor to be considered that was still developing at the time of writing is the move by many organisations towards an ever-quicker release cycle. Historically, many monolithic applications only have a handful of releases per year. With Agile came an expectation that greater numbers of smaller releases provided a better way of working and this trend continues with DevOps[4] and the move towards 'continuous integration' (CI)[5] and 'continuous delivery' (CD).[6]

In many regards, these forms of more regularly delivering software are seen as advantageous. Even information security can generally be in favour of such an approach, as it hopefully means that time to implement fixes for vulnerabilities is decreased. With penetration testing specifically, however, the challenge becomes how to keep up a rate of testing that matches the ever more rapid form of deployment.

It appears clear that increasing amounts of automation of security testing will form at least part of the solution. Wholly automated testing, however, cannot really be considered penetration testing. In terms of means to address this, first, some vendors are starting to offer hybrid services where there are ongoing automated tests, augmented by periodic human intervention to provide additional assurance. Second, more frequent releases typically mean that individual releases are smaller and, as a result, it is possible that only a small number of areas of a system have been changed. It therefore becomes valuable to adopt means of identifying which areas of a system have changed. One such approach is to implement extensive file integrity monitoring (FIM),[7] and to make the output available to testers. By being able to highlight **where** changes have been made, the testing can be more targeted, rather than having to perform a (more time-consuming and costly) complete re-test across areas which definitely have not been altered. Other mechanisms by which this means of demonstrating consistency has been enforced include: the use of containers that are read-only and through the use of CMDB (a configuration management database).

SUMMARY

We have discussed how penetration testing is increasingly becoming seen as a 'must do', as opposed to a 'nice to have' activity. Some of the impacts of tests have been explored, along with some considerations to be made with regards to notifying users of systems that testing is occurring and notifying stakeholders and system owners of the results of the test, their implications and follow up. We have also discussed the need to 'evolve' penetration testing strategies on an ongoing basis perhaps after discovering vulnerabilities and especially after breaches. Perhaps most importantly, it is necessary to ensure that penetration testing is integrated into the broader processes and workflows of the organisation, if it is to be successful, especially as software lifecycles tend to become quicker.

5 OUTCOME- AND INTELLIGENCE-LED PENETRATION TESTING

Jason Charalambous and Moinuddin Zaki

In this chapter we discuss outcome-led penetration testing and intelligence-led penetration testing.

Outcome-led penetration testing relies first on set objectives and outcomes which drive how a penetration test should be carried out, in order to satisfy these objectives.

Intelligence-led penetration testing relies upon contextualised intelligence which defines the attack vectors of an organisation and allows the penetration tests to be positioned from the right angle. The benefit of this is that it provides a structured and effective approach for an organisation to mitigate its actual risks based on its attack vectors and the associated threat landscape that is relevant to their current infrastructure set up and security controls. In the second half of this chapter we explain how penetration tests can be designed to be more targeted and focused to mimic the strategies and approaches used by real-world threat actors based on the intelligence gathered about them.

HOW PENETRATION TEST PROGRAMMES SHOULD BE INFORMED BY DEFINED OUTCOMES

To specify the desired outcomes of a penetration test programme, it is important to be aware of your organisation's functions, infrastructure, area of expertise and goals. This is because one of the primary purposes of a penetration test programme is to meet some (if not all) of the security-related organisational objectives. These objectives are aligned with the organisation's best practices and are employed in order to define and enhance the security in place.

On top of this, the organisation has to establish why a penetration test is required in their case. The reasons why a company would start considering a penetration test can vary from a simple system vulnerability discovery and assessment, to regulatory compliance and customer protection. Different reasons for conducting testing indicate different approaches to a penetration test – and as a result, different outcomes too. By defining outcomes, this leads to:

- The right definition of the scope – if a test is mis-scoped, it will be of limited use or even no use at all.

- The right type of tests – there are lots of different types of penetration tests and using the right ones are vital.

- The time that the tester(s) need to carry out such tests – the scale and complexity of the targets in scope will be impacted based on the set outcomes.

- The allocation of an appropriate budget to enable the management of the project's lifecycle.

'Working back' from defined outcomes to design test programmes

Once the defined outcomes are aligned with the organisational objectives, the client IT team along with the penetration testers have to create the test path that will be followed during penetration testing. The resulting test programme which will be created must not collide with the organisational objectives, and only work alongside them in such a manner that no disruption will be caused.

The testing should be aligned with the reason why the organisation decided a penetration test is required, as this is crucial in defining the methodology used and the resources the organisation is willing to expend.

> By 'resources', we do not only mean the financials of the matter, but also the human resources that will be involved, as well the system resources (for example, one standby engineer and a full clone of the environment, or two engineers while testing the live environment).

Based on defined outcomes and scope of the penetration test, the strategy which will be followed must include involvement of key functions of the organisation as agreed and each individual test should be tailored based on the functionality of every application and system within the scope.

Avoidance of 'scope creep' – and how this can be achieved

'Scope creep' is very common in projects including any penetration testing activity against a set target; it can cause delays in project delivery, meeting the required objectives and pricing, if not addressed in the early stages of the project. This often occurs where the importance of an outcome has not been defined properly or where an outcome has not been aligned with the organisational test objectives and contractual agreements. To be precise, the scope may not have been appropriately defined and agreed by the relevant parties (customer, service providers and other third parties) before any contractual agreement. To eliminate any scope creep the following must always be set in stone before the testing begins:

- Defined starting dates and times.

- Specific IP addresses, network ranges, URLs and domain names. Validation of the target ownership should be carried out to ensure that the scope is not deviating to assets not belonging to the current customer.

- Post-exploitation activities. These must be clearly defined as they tend to go beyond the agreed scope and if they are not controlled they can cause operational issues and legal problems.

Changes to the agreed scope during the execution of the test must be avoided and should be planned at a different time interval; this is because the time needed, the types of tests, the pricing and skillset of testers vary.

The first and most important measure to take to avoid scope creep is for both the organisation and the penetration test team and manager to actually understand the outcomes that have been defined for the penetration testing. By saying this, we are referring to instances where an organisation has stated what it wants, but it actually wants a different result, often due to different interpretations of requirements and their associated objectives between the organisation and the testing company. As a simplified example, X organisation wants to test how good its IT security posture is. While engaging for a penetration test the organisation is trying to say that it wants to see if it can be compromised by any means. However, it only mentions possible compromise via its external-facing web services. In that case, while scoping, the service provider would only consider any online website, portals and so on.

However, what the organisation actually wants is a full-scale penetration test that not only includes testing the externally facing web applications and portals but also the internal systems and digital assets.

There is a clear case of what the business is expecting out of a penetration test (outcome) and what the service provider has understood about the requirements. Straight away, from a seemingly small (comparatively) task of penetration testing the web applications, we went to a full organisational penetration test, as this is what the organisation really wanted from the start. Hence, clearly communicating what exactly is required out of a penetration test, making sure that the business and the service provider clearly understand and are on the same page regarding the desired outcomes can avoid the trouble of adding extra hours and delays in the completion of the testing activity.

The second way to avoid scope creep is to properly define the scope. Although scope should always be agreed upon prior to any penetration testing action being taken, there are often occasions where an organisation has resources that, although they can be used to exploit something within the scope, are actually outside of it.

Third, as in other routine business practices, ensure a framework agreement is in place in writing and the price is agreed in advance. It might sound straightforward, but the agreed price does not only apply to the test programme, but also applies to the reporting, potential patch process, re-testing and so on. If on the initial agreement nothing is specified, it is not always possible to assume what post-activities are included following the report delivery (i.e. re-testing).

THREAT INTELLIGENCE-LED PENETRATION TESTING

Organisations are under tremendous pressure to manage different types of data security-related threats affecting their businesses. Traditional security, if implemented correctly and effectively, can negate many known threats. However, how about the threats that the organisation is unaware of? How does one acquire knowledge about the unknown threats?

As the threat landscape is constantly evolving and different threat actors – unknown, known and new – surface regularly, it becomes imperative for organisations to know who the enemy is – and what their motivations are – to be able to make effective decisions in order to improve their businesses' security posture (SANS Institute, 2005). These questions can be answered by cyber-threat intelligence that can assist organisations in acquiring an up-to-date security posture towards previously unknown threats.

Cyber-threat intelligence has been a buzzword in the information security domain for some time. Simply put, threat intelligence is knowledge. This knowledge contains information about threat actors, the attack vectors they use and the organisations or businesses that are being targeted by them. This information can be highly valuable to any organisation in identifying information security threats targeting their industry and in helping them to make informed decisions to deal with such threats. Threat intelligence can be obtained by threat-intel vendors, which gather customised information relating to an organisation from open and closed forums and sites over the web, but also from sources located in the deep web.

The main goal a normal penetration test tries to achieve is discovering the vulnerabilities and weaknesses within operational and technical components in order to rectify them before a malicious attacker can compromise them. Usually a normal penetration testing service can include running a set of standard tools to test for a series of known vulnerabilities.

As the complexity and the sophistication of cyber attacks is increasing, they are also becoming more focused, targeting specific industries, and their assets.

Some of the existing penetration testing services, though well documented and understood, do not provide enough assurance against more sophisticated attacks on some critical information assets; hence, there arises a need for threat intelligence-based penetration testing.

Threat intelligence-led penetration testing engagements are usually planned and executed together with the client by making use of either the client's threat-based intelligence or that provided by independent third parties. The threat intelligence component within the penetration test will review a variety of known threat actors, and will try to identify those which are more likely to try to achieve their goals by targeting the organisation. This not only requires knowledge about the threats gathered via the threat intelligence feeds but also those from a detailed review of the business's activities and processes.

Once the threats that are most likely to be utilised by attackers are identified, the intelligence information from the feeds can also identify different attack vectors that can be used to attack the organisation. The same attack vectors and intelligence information is then used by the penetration testing team to simulate an attack on the organisation. The goal of threat intelligence-based penetration testing is **not** to find as many vulnerabilities as possible, but to assess how effectively the target organisation is able to detect and respond to simulated attacks.

Advantages of threat intelligence-led penetration testing

So, is the threat-based penetration test better than the normal penetration test? Often penetration tests and threat intelligence-led penetration tests are carried out by the same service provider, using different methods and techniques for different assessments. One is not necessarily better or more advantageous than the other. Each assessment is helpful in certain situations based on the predefined objectives.

It is very important to know the different aims of each type of assessment. A penetration test is mainly used to discover as many vulnerabilities as possible. However, a threat intelligence-based penetration test mainly aims to mimic relevant threats and the threat actors' approach in attacking the organisation while allowing the organisation to assess its incident response processes. Threat intelligence assessments are usually employed as a distinct and defined assessment tool to secure organisations, alongside penetration testing and vulnerability assessments.

There are certainly advantages to the threat intelligence-based penetration tests:

- A much stealthier methodology is employed wherein the organisation targeted is based on profiling done on various threat actors and the vectors they employ.
- It is a very good opportunity to test the real-time incident response capabilities and processes of the organisation.
- It helps in identifying physical, hardware, software and human vulnerabilities.
- It effectively evaluates the robustness of various security controls that are protecting the infrastructure.[1]
- It helps in developing a more relevant and complete security programme for the organisation.

NEXT STEPS?

Although it seems to parallel the activities of real cyber attackers, penetration testing serves, in fact, to alert organisational asset owners to the real dangers present in their systems. It is also imperative for them to know how to use the results of a penetration test to embed best security practices within an organisation. When a certain weakness is identified within an IT system or an application, an effort should be made from the organisation's IT team to analyse:

- What attack vectors led to the exploit?
- What path was taken by the penetration testers to exploit it?
- What holes within other assets helped in the successful exploitation?
- What other IT systems that were not part of the scope of testing could also be exploited?

The answers to the above questions provide very good insight into the processes that need to be reviewed within the organisation. This type of analysis nearly always reveals various holes within the processes that were probably never analysed before the penetration test was conducted.

Just planning a penetration test and fixing the vulnerabilities identified should not be the only achievement of a penetration test – it should never be considered as purely a checkbox exercise to meet certain compliance requirements. Using the penetration test outcomes to fix holes within the various IT and operational processes that the organisation employs goes a long way to improving and optimising the security programme within the organisation.

SUMMARY

Outcome-led penetration testing helps organisations that have a clear understanding of what they expect or what the objectives of a penetration test are in focusing their resources and penetration testing activities particularly on those outcomes. Scope creep is commonly seen within these types of penetration tests where there is a difference between what is expected and the outcome of the test. Effective communication, scope definition and experience in penetration testing can help avoid outcome creep.

Intelligence-led penetration testing is being increasingly adopted by bigger enterprises and recently by even small- and medium-scale enterprises. This type of test increases the boundaries of a classic or conventional penetration by closely mimicking and adopting similar tactics and strategies to those of the threat actors who are persistently targeting critical assets. Intelligence-led penetration testing has huge benefits to an organisation but also comes with an additional cost because of the amount of resources required. This type of penetration testing is a stealthier form of testing where various threat profiles are created and the test is carried out along those attack vectors. This type of test is usually a simulated attack where the effectiveness of security monitoring capabilities may also be evaluated.

REFERENCE

SANS Institute (2005) *Secure Coding: Practical Steps to Defend Your Web Apps.* Available at: https://software-security.sans.org/resources/paper/reading-room/threat-modeling-process-ensure-application-security

6   SCOPING A PENETRATION TEST

Jims Marchang and Roderick Douglas

This chapter considers the scope of a penetration test. The scope will determine which systems should be tested, when and how they may be subjected to tests and any limitations such as systems or networks specifically included or excluded from testing. A clear understanding of the scope of a test is vital both for the organisation being tested and for the tester. Organisations should have a solid idea of which systems and networks they would like to be tested, and what access or information the tester needs to be given in order to complete the penetration testing. Testers need to know what access they have been granted, which tests they are required to perform and any systems or tests specifically required or excluded from testing.

DEFINING THE SCOPE OF PENETRATION TESTS

Defining the scope of a penetration test helps determine what to test, to what extent to test, how long to test and finally the kind of tools required during the test.

Moreover, by defining a scope, the client organisation and the tester will have an agreement on what is permitted to be included in the test and what kinds of vulnerabilities should be focused upon, depending on the needs of the organisation. The scope will guide the penetration testers in engaging within the relevant terms and executing tests with the required precision.

The scope of the penetration test will depend upon the nature of the systems or networks to be tested. The horizon of the test will depend on a variety of factors including the type of system (client or server – if client, then whether it's a thin or a fat client).

A fat or a thick client is a computing system connected in a network with all, or most, resources installed locally, whereas thin clients are those whose resources are distributed over the network.

The nature of the operating system, whether Linux, Windows, Mac or another will influence the nature of testing to be performed, as different operating systems have different known vulnerabilities and required security patches which may determine testing procedures. The testing scope will also be governed by the nature in which the systems are connected to a network. In a large network, it may be viable to test only a specific section of the network, or selected ports as a sample, when the configuration of the entire network is the same.

The focus of the test for vulnerabilities may thus begin by considering:

- the system's architecture;
- operating system(s) being run;
- the application design type and application platform;
- ways of communication;
- the nature of data;
- deployment nature of the systems;
- available security features of the system;
- the security settings used by the systems.

The scope of the test will also be defined by the information available about the system and amount of information provided to the tester, so that the tester can set the right goals and approach using an appropriate methodology. The scope of the penetration test therefore must align with the purpose of the test, when it will be carried out, how it will be carried out, the duration of the test and the reports to be generated from the test (Penetration Test Guidance Special Interest Group PCI Security Standards Council, 2015).

It is the scope that makes a penetration test meaningful and realistic.

Actions related to the planning, execution and post-execution of penetration testing should also be defined in a scope (Scarfone et al., 2008).

In a penetration test, unless the scope is defined, it will be hard to project or know for sure the boundaries to be tested. However, the effectiveness of the test and the scope of the test will be governed by other factors including time, complexity of the test, availability of the information and accessibility of the system to the tester, and finally the expertise of the tester. Let's look at an example.

The Payment Card Industry Data Security Standard (PCI DSS) defines the cardholder data environment (CDE) as 'the people, processes, and technology that store, process, or transmit cardholder data or sensitive authentication data' (Penetration Test Guidance Special Interest Group PCI Security Standards Council, 2015, p. 4).

As it deals with sensitive transaction-related information, the scope of a penetration test for PCI DSS systems should be extensive and include both internal (the system's design, architecture, internal storage, applications running in the internal network among others) and external (connections from external networks to internal servers, services, firewall, access ports and so on) penetration testing, exploring all vulnerabilities and assessing any unique access from the public network, private network or remote access using a virtual private network (VPN) or dial-up connection.

Threat intelligence

According to BAE Systems, penetration testing services can be 'more targeted and focussed' if the organisational assets which might warrant an attack and the possible perpetrators and attack vectors are first considered (BAE Systems Applied Intelligence, 2015, p. 3). Such considerations will affect the agreed scope of penetration testing.

Acquiring specific threat intelligence prior to penetration testing will be useful and will help the tester to be more focused and able to link actual flaws with the organisation. However, the interests and targets of attackers are dynamic in nature, so while focusing on the scope based on the inputs provided by threat intelligence, the penetration tester could miss other areas of vulnerabilities. Care should be taken to avoid this.

The security needs of an organisation can vary, and due to the nature of the execution, processing and communication of a system, the vulnerability and cyber-attack issues will also fluctuate. Depending on the services provided and supported by the organisation, there might be ways to avoid unnecessary tests by not conducting tests for services that are not available, to save time, effort and money. For example, if an organisation's internal file server is activated and made operational only within the internal organisation systems, and its firewalls do not allow a VPN for remote access, then penetration testing from an external network to access a local file server can be avoided. By considering the threat intelligence information and the nature of the system, a fixed budget can also be allocated to focus only on those relevant vulnerable areas.

When a scope is defined based on organisational need and known vulnerabilities, then the required skillset for a penetration tester can be identified easily, the right expertise can be included in the team depending on the amount of work to be handled and an agreed time frame can be proposed.

MAPPING OF ASSETS

In order to understand what to test, on what to test and how to test, it is important to first map the assets of the organisation. The scope of penetration testing can then cover all the aspects of testing necessary, irrespective of the kinds of devices, version of the devices, version of the system software, version of application or types of operating system running in the computers, switches or routers of the network.

The assets of an organisation can broadly be classified into **human resources**, in terms of staffing, skills and so on, and **infrastructure**, in terms of systems, networks and bandwidth. Insight into the hierarchical organisational structure of human resources will help in understanding what can be accessed by whom and thus in drafting the structure of the scope to test, taking what can be accessed at what level into consideration. The mapping of assets in terms of infrastructure will enlighten those who prepare the penetration testing scope in ensuring that no errant systems or networks are overlooked; without this, it will also be hard to understand the possibility of vulnerabilities that could exist because of diverse systems and versions running in different devices in the network.

IT practitioners should use a validated asset inventory to represent the data repositories, data flow, and infrastructure and network connectivity within their organisations (Beveridge et al., 2016). It is vital to manage systems and data, based on their level of criticality to the organisation, the sensitivity of the information, dependencies of data across the systems or networks, point of contact, roles and responsibilities (Creasey and Glover, 2017). The connection, data flow and dependency between the users and the network components of an example organisation are shown in Figure 6.1.

Figure 6.1 Network components, data flow and user connection in an example organisation

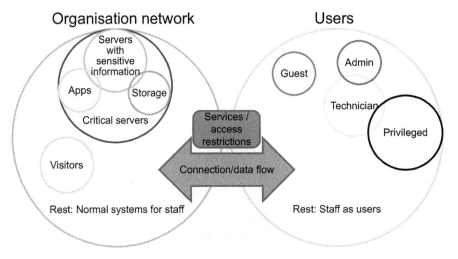

It is important that those preparing the testing scope have access to a record of all known malicious behaviour on the network and a record of all security settings; this, in white-box testing, provides the penetration tester with useful insight.

The asset mapping and relevant system documentation should also provide vital information about:

- the network architecture;
- types of hardware running in each system;
- types of operating system used;
- types of application running in each system;
- the role of each system in terms of being a client or a server;
- possible vulnerabilities;
- the existing security measures and adopted security settings.

When records are maintained by an organisation, it is crucial that the relationship between organisational data, business needs and how the needs are satisfied is understood. If the IT practitioners do not understand or know the dependency between the technology used in processing, storing, sharing or transferring the data in line with business needs, then the information is at risk of being lost, tampered with or stolen. When the technology used in an organisation is not fully known, then there is a high risk of even losing the ability to access, locate, open, work with, understand and trust organisational data (The National Archives, 2017). Mapping the technical dependencies of the infrastructure and other technical environments with the information flowing in the network of an organisation will enable the users or administrator, or anyone responsible, to manage the risk more efficiently. It will also be easier to manage the impact of change, any upgrade, overcome vulnerabilities and ultimately help in protecting the entire network.

An example mapping of the technical environment of a network infrastructure is shown in Figure 6.2. With the help of such documentation it will be easier for penetration testers to focus on and conduct the required tests based on the testing scope and its need to protect the network as well as the information flowing in the network.

Figure 6.2 Mapping the technical environment to understand the network infrastructure

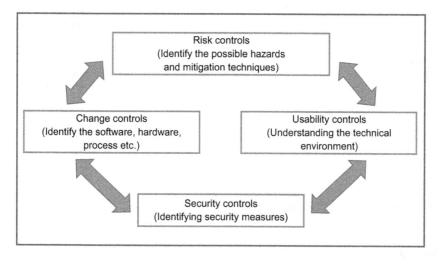

Networks and technologies keep evolving, so what is secure now may not be a secure system in the future. To ensure a secure system, it is important to retain all documentation related to all the systems and network dependencies, and any details of the network environment to ease upgrade, integration, investigation process and in finding any loopholes.

During an investigation process or during a review of network monitoring, it is highly likely that new assets in terms of hardware or software may be discovered which are not in the documentation. Such systems may have been unrecorded because they:

• are due to a new installation;

• may be an old system which was forgotten about in the recording process;

• may be an old system which was forgotten and should have been removed;

• might have been placed, installed or connected into the network by an intruder.

When a new, unrecorded asset is discovered, then detailed investigation needs to be conducted before recording it. By doing so, any form of anomaly can be discovered. If it is a new installation, then the detailed specification and its role should be recorded and can be included during the penetration test. If it is discovered to be unknown software it should be removed or uninstalled.

During the investigation for a penetration test, it is not necessary to conduct a test for every aspect of an organisation's IT assets, but rather focus on certain key assets, based on organisational requirements. Moreover, it is also important to record any system that is not tested when it is out of the scope and the reasons why.

SUMMARY

The scope of penetration testing is vital in mending all the possible vulnerabilities and loopholes in a network, devices attached to the network and the services running on the devices. It is the scope that defines what to test and how to test and so on, so it is important to provide the range and the boundaries to the penetration testers. Moreover, gathering threat intelligence before deciding on the scope provides a better platform in framing the scope of the testing and making the test more successful.

In preparing a penetration testing scope, it is vital to have a record of all the assets and dependencies of an organisation, their technical attributes, who uses them, who owns them, who supports them or who will support them in future. Any new or old unrecorded assets should be recorded, and documentation should be carried out by a skilled IT professional for future reference.

REFERENCES

BAE Systems Applied Intelligence (2015) *Intelligence-Led Penetration Testing Services*. Guildford, UK: BAE Systems Applied Intelligence.

Beveridge, C., Pinckard, J.L., Rattigan, M. and Vrtis, R.A. (2016) *A Mapping of the Federal Financial Institutions Examination Council (FFIEC) Cybersecurity Assessment Tool (CAT) to the Cyber Resilience Review (CRR)*. Pittsburgh, PA: Software Engineering Institute.

Creasey, J. and Glover, I. (2017) *A Guide for Running an Effective Penetration Testing Programme*. Slough, UK: CREST.

Penetration Test Guidance Special Interest Group PCI Security Standards Council (2015) *Information Supplement: Penetration Testing Guidance*. Wakefield, MA: PCI Data Security Standards Council.

Scarfone, K., Souppaya, M., Cody, A. and Orebaugh, A. (2008) *Technical Guide to Information Security Testing and Assessment*. NIST Special Publication no. 800-115. Gaithersburg, MD: National Institute of Standards and Technology.

The National Archives (2017) *Mapping the Technical Dependencies of Information Assets*. Kew, UK: The National Archives.

7 PENETRATION TEST COVERAGE AND SIMULATING THE THREAT

Felix Ryan

Penetration tests need to be structured correctly, with good coverage, and should be undertaken for a useful purpose. This chapter delves into a number of topics that will make it easier to create good penetration test coverage and a simulation that aligns with the threat to the organisation and system.

PENETRATION TEST COVERAGE AND STRUCTURE

Test coverage is critical in ensuring that the penetration testing exercise being completed is done to a standard that makes it worthwhile. This section looks at several elements that will help you to ensure you get the correct penetration test coverage for your organisation's needs.

Selecting a target for penetration testing

It is not possible to prepare perfectly for an entire security test. There are, however, a few items that can be completed that will make the experience a lot smoother, and help in getting the most out of the exercise.

Start by working with each department in the organisation and establishing a list of all the assets they manage, have dependencies on or interact with. This list should not just include those that have the most impact on the organisation, but should include those assets that they are less worried about as well.

All the organisational assets will need testing at some point to gain assurance that it isn't possible to break into a less-important system in order to then gain access to a highly valued system. With all these systems, also list the technical details that identify them; for example, with a web application test, this might be a particular IP address, domain name or URL, while an internal network test might identify the IP address of the server, along with the network within which the system is located.

Each of the items on the asset list should be considered for the level of risk the system poses to the organisation. This calculation can be brief, as it only needs to provide a prioritisation. To make this calculation, consider the:

- number of security tests that have been completed against the target;
- perceived capabilities of the system developers;

- sensitivity and value of the data being stored, transmitted or processed; and

- level of exposure this system has to its potential threat actors.

The second thing you will need to do is establish a budget. If budgets get handed down from top-level management and it is the first penetration test for the organisation, take whatever budget is on offer, as subsequent penetration tests will have the evidence in place to fight for a more appropriate budget. The person that has responsibility for setting the budget should start by understanding the current market's day-rate. Following that, a broad understanding of the size and complexity of the organisation at a very high level is important. It may not be possible to then convert this size and complexity into an estimate of how many weeks of work there are regarding penetration testing, but it should be possible to understand whether there is very little tech to be tested or a lot. Whatever budget is determined, it will soon become clear whether it is enough for an ongoing programme or even for a single test. The good news is that in reality even a small budget will at least get you a basic test, and will probably give the organisation some knowledge of areas in need of corrective actions.

Test duration and scheduling

Timing and scheduling are in reference to the duration of a penetration test exercise, and the times and dates when a test will start and finish.

When it comes to test duration, there are two types of test: sampled and exhaustive. The trade-off between the two is test duration (budget) versus assurance gained. If the test is exhaustive it will cover all areas, thus taking longer; but at the same time providing a higher level of assurance. The inverse is true for sampled tests; however, that does not mean that a degree of sampling should be avoided. There are obvious limits to the efficacy of sampling: too little coverage is like sniffing cheese from 10 feet away – only the worst smelling targets will be noticed; while if sampling 95% of the target, the last bit may as well be eaten so it isn't lonely in the fridge.

Test duration will ultimately be dictated by the budget for the exercise; however, where there is a choice to be had, the length of the test duration should be proportional to the size of the target. For example, if the exercise is a web application test and the web application only has one function, it might be considered very small, in which case the test may only take two or three days. If the web application has a large number of complex functions, it might be considered very large in which case the test duration will need to be much longer – maybe even several weeks. If there is not that much time, take on a testing team as they will be able to cut down the overall test duration by working in parallel.

At the time of writing there is a shortage of personnel in the security testing industry; this shortage means that diary availability for penetration testers can be a challenge. It is not uncommon to experience lead times of three months before a tester is available. The key here is to book the penetration test as early as is feasible, particularly if there are deadlines to be achieved. If the project requires penetration testing in a very short time frame it might be possible to get several testers to each perform a very small number of days to build up to the overall number of days that has been chosen for the required level of assurance. This tactic will provide some results; however, it is important to understand that it is an inefficient use of time owing to handing the project over between testers, and will not necessarily give good results as it is very difficult to be certain that the correct coverage has been completed. Where this method of calendar juggling is a must, try to fit in an extra day or two to compensate.

Testing can be commissioned for long-standing systems as well as those that are being developed or implemented. For those long-standing systems, it is probably sensible to not schedule a penetration test of it within a few months of it being decommissioned. There is nothing more demoralising for a penetration tester to be told at the beginning of the exercise than 'I'm not really sure why you're testing that... we turn it off in a few weeks'.

There are two elements that should be considered when a project is being developed or implemented: scheduling penetration testing so that it doesn't delay the launch of the project and having security advice and testing built into the entire development or implementation timeline. It is much more efficient to get insight into the security of a system as it is being developed or implemented rather than risk having to make major changes once it is complete.

Supplier and client assurance

Client assurance is the process whereby an organisation attempts to produce evidence to assure its clients that the organisation's systems, either specific to the client's interest or the entirety of the organisation, are secure. This is a common driver for penetration testing, and can have an impact on the methods, conditions and frequency of penetration testing, as well as how nervous the organisation commissioning the test is about the results.

In 2013 the American retail organisation Target was breached by hackers via one of Target's heating, ventilation and air conditioning (HVAC) suppliers. It is believed that the initial access in this breach was completed by using a phishing email against an employee of the HVAC supplier. The phishing attack then allowed the attacker to install a password harvesting tool which compromised a password that belonged to Target's vendor access portal. The event was heavily publicised at the time and in the years following there has been significant analysis of what actually happened and how repeat incidents could be prevented. One such study by the SANS Institute (Radichel, 2019) discusses, among other areas, requirements that could have been made by Target on its suppliers. It's fair to say that the vast majority of preventive actions that could have been taken lie with Target itself; however, strong supplier assurance could potentially have prevented the breach as well. For example, the SANS report suggests that requiring the supplier to have fully functioning anti-malware software would have prevented the password harvesting tool from being installed. However, note that infrastructure penetration test reports often include findings about the ineffectiveness of anti-malware products. This is particularly the case when those defensive technologies fail to detect the malware payloads used by the penetration testers that are generated by open-source tools.

Anti-malware products are considered as only one component within a defence-in-depth approach to information security. The anti-malware tools that are considered the most effective by security experts change year-on-year owing to the fact that the tools that create malware are constantly under development specifically to defeat the latest and best anti-malware functionality. Fundamentally, this is an arms race and it is difficult to keep up to date on both sides of the battle. These products absolutely have their place, but where they are used they must be configured correctly and their users must have reasonable expectations of their abilities.

When dealing with client assurance, the choice of penetration testing conditions and sampling may not be under the organisation's control; it may be set by some form of client pressure that is specific to the type of client. For example, if the organisation works for a government body, that government body may specify the frequency, scope and depth of penetration testing that they require the client to have completed. In that case, the contract will dictate and prescribe the situation, and instead it becomes a case of understanding exactly what is required.

When you are required to provide assurance to clients make sure that the level of detail the client requires is understood, and what scope is important to them. For example, providing them with an executive summary and issuing summary tables is often considered enough, as they demonstrate the level of security without giving away so much detail that the client would be able to cause a breach. If the organisation is receiving assurance from its clients, this works in reverse: check the scope coverage and consider what level of detail is appropriate.

It can be difficult dealing with the consequences of admitting to the client that security falls short of requirements. Most of the time I experience or hear about client relationships that have been constructive and pragmatic. This is where realistic and pertinent questions are asked and then an agreement is sought which specifies realistic deadlines. Every now and then, however, I have also come across entirely unreasonable situations, where the third-party client is demanding that everything is fixed by the organisation within a very short time frame, including the items that have been deemed low-risk. This is clearly going to be down to the strength and characteristics of the relationship between organisation and client. One observation this author has had in those challenging circumstances, is that often, the unreasonable demands were made as a result of misunderstandings or lack of knowledge on the relevant technologies and vulnerabilities involved. Clearly this works both ways round; if you are looking for your clients to provide assurance on information security, make sure appropriate deadlines and goals are set; after all, it isn't possible to be 100% secure, as the situation is constantly changing.

External conflicts of interest

It is generally accepted that penetration testers should not test any corrective actions that they have taken on behalf of their clients. This is too much like marking the penetration tester's own work, which is ethically questionable at best and potentially dangerously misleading at worst. This is because there are opportunities for a conflict of interest, some more obvious than others. For example, the tester gets to charge twice, once to find the problem and then again to fix it – but if no one else sees or understands the problem, how can it be validated that the problem was there in the first place?

Such a conflict of interest does not simply apply to the individual tester; it might apply to the penetration test service provider itself. For example, does the supplier do anything else for the organisation, such as any managed services? Are its individual test consultants in a different department from those that are performing other services for the organisation? Do not automatically rule out situations like this: there may be rivalries, where one team actively wants to break the work of another team which might result in some good findings. Furthermore, if one team finds a problem, the other team is going to struggle to argue that it doesn't need fixing without a serious amount of internal debate.

If you find yourself in a difficult situation where a split needs to be established, there is a trusted adage within the world of information security known as Schneier's Law (Schneier, 2011): 'any person can invent a security system so clever that she or he can't think of how to break it'. This phrase is most commonly used in reference to encryption algorithms; however, it actually applies to the whole information security domain. This law was named after Bruce Schneier, by Cory Doctorow (2004), but it is believed that originally this was a concept coined by Charles Babbage.[1] Essentially, it means that it takes more than one perspective to be able to conclude that a system works in the way intended and is secure. In the context of a security test and its practical application, this law states that the individuals who built a system's security defences can't be the same as those who test those security defences.

Should there even be small indicators of a moral or ethical problem pertaining to the penetration testing programme, get to the bottom of it before it becomes something serious. Hopefully the issue will be far less significant than first thought and progress can be made, but if there is an issue, resolve it as early as possible, before it is too late.

Internal conflicts of interest

When acting as a team receiving the outcomes of a penetration testing exercise, there are likely to be a range of emotions present. Be careful not to bring a conflict of interest to discussions, and help those having a conflict of interest to consciously realise this, so that they can direct their energy appropriately. Sometimes these lines can blur and it is no longer clear what the situation is; the chances are, though, that the penetration tester just wants their work to be representative and accurate.

There are two main types of conflict of interest. These aren't official terms but here they are named 'suppressive' and 'promotive'. Suppressive conflicts of interest are where the outcome of the exercise is minimised in order to reduce the perceived impact. This can be risky because the legitimate problems may get swept under the carpet and remain vulnerable. Promotive conflicts of interest are where the drive is to make everything sound terrible in order to achieve a particular goal. This can be risky as those receiving the information could criticise the outcomes of the exercise as unnecessarily inflammatory, and also question its accuracy or entirely discredit the outcomes.

One example of a vested and clearly suppressive conflict of interest is where a product manager wants a solution to pass a penetration test: they may push the tester to downgrade vulnerability scores, as in their eyes a poor report will prevent them from making the system live. Equally, an example of a vested interest which is more subtly suppressive-conflicted is the engineer that created the product wanting to downgrade the severity of the vulnerability scores because they spent hours on the code and are proud of their efforts.

Promotive conflicts of interest can be harder to discern. An example is where there is a desire to increase the severity rating of one or two reported vulnerabilities. The tester may never know the cause of this, but it might be something simple such as gaining extra budget because 'things are bad', or something very specific and complex, such as building a dismissal case against a member of staff.

Size and frequency of penetration test exercises

The security world moves constantly, every day new issues, risks, weaknesses, attack techniques and vulnerabilities are made and published. It is possible to go from having a rose-coloured world one day, to being on an emergency conference call the next morning because a new vulnerability has been released. From a penetration testing perspective, the challenge of this perpetual motion is ensuring that there is adequate coverage of all current problems as well as the entire back catalogue of possible vulnerabilities.

All organisations have the flexibility of choosing the frequency of their penetration tests, but some have minimum requirements imposed upon them from external sources such as regulations, client assurance or standards compliance. Aside from these external pressures, there is no hard and fast rule for the frequency of penetration tests. It is common for annual penetration tests to occur on systems that are not actively being developed and for any significant changes to be subjected to a penetration test immediately after they have been completed. That said, the frequency with which penetration tests should be completed is best guided by the context and risk appetite of the organisation and the systems being tested.

Organisations talk about detecting 'low-hanging fruit': the quick-and-easy fixes that would otherwise give their attackers an opportunity to exploit. This analogy works, but only in the context of a single testing exercise, because low-hanging fruit grows over time. This analogy still has significance though, as the majority of the harvesting of low-hanging fruit will occur in the first few testing exercises. After this, those big hitters will become fewer and further apart.

This begs the question 'what next?' and the answer is to decide whether more depth is appropriate. There are lots of reasons why more depth might be desirable: for example, the system might hold very sensitive data or be used by very high-profile clients and so on. Overall though, it is important to realise that just because a test programme took eight days last year does not mean it is fixed at eight days; for instance, it might be desirable for it to take 10 days this year.

Organisation size

The size of the organisation has a significant impact on how penetration testing is performed, not only from a coverage perspective, but also with respect to how a threat is simulated. In reality, threat actors have as much time as they want, which means they can attempt to attack as much or as little of a targeted organisation's infrastructure as they want. This might sound like test coverage should always be 100 per cent of the attack surface regardless of the size of the organisation, known as 'exhaustive testing'.

In an ideal world this is the case; but it is rare for this ideal situation to occur. This is where sampling comes in. Sampling has two main forms: vulnerability-class sampling and system sampling.

Vulnerability-class sampling is where the penetration tester does not try to exhaustively find every single instance of a particular vulnerability, but instead attempts to find one of each type, or classification, of vulnerability in each system. This type of sampling works best for web applications or other custom-built applications.

System sampling is where the scope is limited to a representative sample of systems and instead requires the tester to find as many different instances of problems that they can, no matter how repetitive or diverse.

For both types, following the tester's report and educational activities, it then becomes the organisation's responsibility to find and fix every instance of the problem. It might sound like this is the best solution for larger organisations or those with a constrained budget; it certainly helps, but the organisation must fundamentally understand that they are taking at least one risk. With vulnerability-class sampling, the risk is that the client will not be able to find all instances of the problem and will not recognise the more advanced and edge-case versions of the same problem. While system sampling, on the other hand, carries the risk that the representative sample is not actually representative, and that there is variation, for example, between office locations (which means one office is more vulnerable than the others).

Furthermore, a sampled test must be acceptable for whatever purpose the test is to fulfil. For example, client assurance or contractual obligations might require exhaustive testing. Some testers might also provide a certificate of achievement for those tests that are exhaustive and contain no concerning vulnerabilities: if this is important to the organisation, make sure the test is suitable for this purpose.

If the organisation is on the larger side, it may be appropriate to allow an exhaustive reconnaissance exercise to be completed. This will enable the organisation to understand how exposed it is to external threat, potentially identify systems that were hidden or otherwise unknown, and therefore make it possible to define an appropriate testing exercise.

There is a sweet spot in terms of security capability that is related to the size of the organisation. Table 7.1 outlines how the approach to enterprise penetration testing needs to be adjusted to suit organisation size and is based upon the author's observations and experience. There are always exceptions to the observations shown in Table 7.1, but so far there have been few and they have usually been to the extreme.

SIMULATING THE THREAT

When designing a penetration testing programme, one of the defining elements will be an estimation of who the threat actors are and how they operate. This estimate should be taken regarding the target to be tested, as well as the overall size and sector of the

Table 7.1 Security capability related to size of organisation

Size of organisation	Very small	Small/medium	Large and very large
Effect on: frequency of testing	Completed infrequently	Testing is performed at appropriate intervals	Regular and frequent testing is possible, though not always completed owing to internal politics
Effect on: which vulnerabilities are dealt with	Extreme and low-hanging fruit results are dealt with, but more advanced vulnerabilities often persist	Results are dealt with to the level at which the company feels comfortable	Results are dealt with to a greater extent, owing to reduced risk appetite
Effect on: speed of fixes being deployed	Commonly a lack of in-house expertise prevents fixes from being produced without external help. External help may be hindered by budgetary constraints	Fixes can be published and put live relatively quickly	The required changes can take a significant time to be pushed into production
Effect on: test sampling	Exercises are forced into sampling owing to budgetary constraints	Exhaustive testing is possible if chosen by the organisation	Exercises are forced into sampling, owing to volume of the information assets
Root cause	Unlikely to have the resources or expertise to identify the problems the organisation faces or ability to deal with them. May not understand the systems that they have that require testing	Enough expertise and resources in order to identify the problems faced and deal with them	No matter how much resource or expertise is thrown at information security, it can be difficult to prevent the internal politics and processes, and the sheer scale of the problem from continuing to outpace the security capabilities of the organisation. Unlikely to know what systems exist that require testing

organisation. By way of example, consider a retail banking group. This organisation might have the following threat actors:

- nation-state sponsored (for example, economic warfare);
- organised crime syndicates;
- staff and third-party suppliers;
- consumers.

The behaviour of each threat actor varies according to their intent, resources and level of access. As you can imagine, testing for security considerations to defend against nation-state sponsored attacks can be somewhat more involved than testing for protecting against errant consumers trying to get something for free. This section examines elements of penetration tests that have an impact on the ability of the penetration test supplier to accurately simulate the threat and what can be done to compensate.

Pre-test 'hygiene' checks

Pre-test hygiene checks are those which make sure no serious problems are present before a test gets under way.

As obvious as this might sound, one of the most important checks that should be completed before any penetration testing begins is whether systems actually work as they are supposed to. Ultimately, the test service provider is being paid for their time, and not the results. To derive the most value from your budget, make sure that testers are able to get started as soon as possible when the testing time frame starts. This goes wrong surprisingly often, and in most circumstances it happens with web applications that are actively being developed.

Part of whether the system works as it is supposed to, is making sure that when the tester runs a given function it outputs data that is realistic and as expected. That is not to say it should be real data – in fact, in a test system it probably shouldn't be – however, the data should be 'lifelike'. This makes it clear to the penetration tester how the system is supposed to behave, and it will assist them in developing attacks that actually make sense in the context of the real system.

Software knowledge

Software knowledge is simply where a penetration tester has prior experience of or knowledge on a particular system, whether that is software or hardware.

When working with all the asset owners you may identify unusual systems. If this is the case, choose penetration testers with this in mind. This can include industrial control systems, mainframes, legacy systems or applications written in obscure programming languages. If the tester has knowledge of these systems they will be more efficient with their testing, and may find vulnerabilities that a less-experienced tester would not identify. The penetration test discipline is already very specialised, so if you add a requirement for even more specialism the cost of the service will likely increase.

Aside from these obvious specialisations, it is less important that the testing consultants are experts in the organisation's particular network, firewall stack, operating system choice and so on. This is because the most important part of a testing exercise is the creative thinking and this is vendor-neutral. Where vendor-specific vulnerabilities need to be tested, the research part of every penetration test will pick these aspects up and check against databases of known vulnerabilities.

Level of information security maturity

Information security maturity is the measure of how advanced an organisation is in its approach to securing its data assets. Often, a high level of maturity comes with many years of dealing with information security issues and embedding appropriate activities within the standard organisational operations. There are several different security maturity models, but ultimately, they refer to the same general principles. Gartner's security maturity model (Scholtz and Heiser, 2013) uses five levels:

- Initial;
- Developing;
- Defined;
- Managed;
- Optimising.

Each of these models represents an improvement of the business's capabilities, but also shows a shift from tactical focus to strategic focus.

During the development of the organisation's information security maturity, testing exercises will change and become a smoother experience. Early testing exercises are typically very exciting, and will be very loosely constrained. This allows the penetration tester to focus on and advise on the areas that present the most opportunities for an attacker. Typically, this means that the range of the test will be very large, covering a bit of everything. Conversely, the size of the exercise is likely to be very small in terms of the number of days allocated. This is often because of budgetary constraints and penetration testers can be left with the impression that the organisation is 'sticking its toes into the water'. Once the organisation has climbed the maturity model ladder, tests can become narrowly focused on a particular system, and are permitted to go into much more depth as a result of having a significant number of days allocated.

Not breaking things

Penetration testing service providers do not want to break things – at least, not in a permanently damaging kind of way. Most penetration testers have a strong moral compass and the act of damaging something goes against this. The motivation behind most of what penetration testers do is twofold. First, they think what they do is cool, exciting and interesting and the more advanced an attack is, the more impressive it is. And second, that by exposing these weaknesses, it makes it possible for them to be corrected and when that happens, the world is that little bit safer.

That said, accidents and unexpected consequences do happen, so wherever possible, arrange testing with this in mind – whether that is a full test system so that breakages simply do not matter or having a dedicated member of staff available for the test duration who can pick up the pieces should anything go wrong. Another tactic is to perform testing outside of standard business hours in order to have as minimal an effect as possible should the worst happen. This is a sensible precaution if there is a lot at stake; however, this will substantially increase the cost of any testing exercise.

The best thing to do is to have a rough plan of action ready should there be problems with a test. This should include lines of communication with the tester, and have enough logging in place to be able to identify the issue, diagnose the problem and implement a fix to get services back online. This logging should also try to provide a method of positively identifying that the cause of the attack actually came from the tester: there is nothing worse than not knowing whether the problem was from a real-life attacker or from the authorised penetration tester. Just a couple of examples of attributes that can identify the attacker are source IP addresses and authentication details such as usernames, passwords and session IDs.

I once had the unfortunate experience of discovering that a client had a Denial of Service (DoS) condition on one of their systems that resides in a different country. During a routine vulnerability scan the scanner sent a standard set of packets to a node in a hypervisor cluster. This node had a misconfiguration, a large number of missing patches and an already very high load, and the scanning packets resulted in the machine freezing. Unfortunately, the virtual machines didn't manage to transfer from one cluster node to the other, as would normally happen in a high-availability cluster, which meant that the machines were stuck in an unknown state. Eventually, the organisation's technicians managed to recover the virtual machine disks and brought them online on a different cluster node. There was panic at the time, as the offline machines equated to a reasonable amount of revenue per hour. It was only owing to the level of logging that I had in place that we could positively identify that it was the scanner's actions that had caused the outage. It wasn't a fun experience; however, once the dust had settled the client was extremely grateful that I had found that problem as it transpired that all its cluster nodes around the world were affected to some degree or other.

Another of my colleagues once found a function in a web application which on the surface was benign, simply executing an SQL statement that removes a comment from a particular profile. However, when it was provided with an incomplete set of parameters, the system matched the empty parameter with every record in that particular table in the database. It was identified later that the system had been programmed to include wildcards which, purely by happenstance, had previously never been known to match anything other than the correct record. Unfortunately, the system being tested was the production system, so for a brief time, all the comments from all profiles on this web application had been destroyed. The good news in this case was that there was a backup in place, and it didn't take long to restore.

Consultant penetration testers are paid to test the limits of the security of a given target. Things going awry are an occupational hazard and should not come as a surprise. When experiencing one of these unfortunate moments with a tester, remember that the organisation has paid for the test, and it is important that both organisations use the incident as a learning point to either prevent it from being a problem, or to get it treated differently the next time the system is tested. Think of employing a penetration test service provider as **managing** risk, not **eliminating** it. There is a risk being taken that something might go wrong; however, it is far less impactful when done in controlled conditions than when a real attacker wants to cause harm.

It is always possible that a real attack will happen at the same time as a penetration test. Do not get complacent. If a penetration test is happening and an alert pops up it is always sensible to verify the finding both from a defensive stand point and from the penetration testers' perspective: they will want to know if you would have ordinarily spotted any of their activities. But don't just go to the testing consultant and tell them that a system saw what they were up to; go with some detail that illuminates what the activity was and the source IP addresses or other available identifying mark. This makes it possible for the tester to confirm that the observed activity was in fact them.

Targeted and untargeted exercises

Targeted exercises are where the penetration testers are provided with a specific scope at the beginning of the engagement before any work is completed, whereas untargeted exercises require the testers to discover the targets. In both examples, the testers will need a confirmed scope before they actually start testing. Typically, an untargeted exercise will use open-source information to try to build up a picture of the infrastructure and services that belong to the organisation, as well as attempting to find members of staff and other assets.

Choosing between these styles very much depends on the objectives of the exercise and the budget available. If the objective is to form an impression of the level of risk a whole organisation has that is as close to 'true life' as possible, then it would be useful to explore the level of discoverability the organisation has in an untargeted exercise. Clearly though, the time that such discovery tasks take will be charged by the testers, which means the budget needs to be larger.

Where the exercise is testing a single, distinct system, there is often little point in running anything other than a targeted test as the risk profile may not change at all depending on how easy or difficult it is to discover. For example, a system that controls the buying and selling of financial assets such as stocks and shares is a high-value target so needs to be strongly resilient to attack in all circumstances.

By way of another example, a company operates a popular consumer-focused web application: the fact that it is in the public domain and is popular means that the assumption should be that it, in its entirety, the web app is going to be discoverable.

Black-box, white-box and grey-box exercises

Penetration testing can be differentiated as black-box, white-box or grey-box testing.

Black-box testing is where testing starts with a broad description of the target, a confirmation of scope when requested and, depending on the circumstances and what threat simulation is being performed, a low-privilege user account's login details. This last point particularly relates strongly to testing web applications. Black-box testing can lead to very creative forms of attack being formed; however, it can result in an exhaustive test being longer than other types.

White-box testing is far less adversarial and involves providing information that a legitimate attacker would not have immediate access to. This could include source-code, API (application programming interface) documentation, network diagrams, database access, firewall rule sets and so on. White-box testing is mostly used for distinct systems, rather than whole organisations, that are actively being developed, as it allows the developers to gain a high level of assurance on a particular product. White-box testing works well for finding difficult to spot technical vulnerabilities, such as certain types of SQL injection, and is often very time-efficient. However, for these same reasons, it can result in reduced consideration for how the features fit together and how the system or service can be used in a perfectly legitimate way to perform tasks that it was not designed for.

Grey-box testing is white-box and black-box testing blended together. This can be as simple as running a black-box test for the first half of the exercise and then a white-box test immediately afterwards for the second half of the exercise. It can also range to the very complex, where each request for information is considered based on the current circumstances and a decision is made to permit or deny the request. Depending on the circumstances, some form of blended exercise is the most thorough and gives the highest level of assurance – but comes with the largest price tag.

IPS, WAF and other active defence systems

Intrusion prevention systems (IPS), web application firewalls (WAFs) and other active defence systems such as port-scan prevention technologies, are methods of preventing known 'bad' actions from happening. They look for these recognisable actions and don't just alert when they see them, but actually respond defensively, preventing the attack from happening.

These technologies are good ways to add to the level of security present in a given system; however, they are just an extra layer of security, not guaranteed safeguards. If these technologies are in place for a penetration test, the only discovery is how good the IPS, WAF or other security technology is, not how good the security is of the actual target. That is not to say that testing a system when it is behind one of these technologies should never be done, just that it should be understood and only done when it is appropriate.

It is probably inappropriate to test a system that is behind an active defence system when the system being tested is still actively supported by the vendor or actively being developed. This is because the test will likely result in many false-negative results, and will make it hard for the penetration tester to find the more advanced attack techniques. Furthermore, the test might actually take longer to complete the same amount of coverage: several of the active defence techniques involve blocking users who make large numbers of requests. This either forces the cost of the test up, or reduces the coverage of the target system. This describes the clear majority of systems: most tests should be carried out without any active defence technology in place between the tester and the target system.

There is one circumstance in particular in which it is appropriate to test with active defences in place: when the system cannot be upgraded or is no longer in active development and cannot be replaced or decommissioned. This represents a risk that the organisation is carrying and can do little about, so performing a penetration testing exercise against it in its strongest configuration will allow the business to better understand that risk.

Input from alerting and monitoring systems

Those companies that have greater information security maturity may have alerting and log monitoring systems in place. A penetration test is a good test of the incident response procedures followed when an alert is raised, but does not indicate that the alerting and monitoring itself is effective. This is because a penetration test is typically a very short engagement over a few weeks compared with a real attack that could take place over many months.

Expect alerts to be triggered in simulated exercises; if they are not then there may be a fundamental problem with the alerting and monitoring technology. Hopefully they will trigger, because what happens next is of most interest. The level of refinement and detail that you want to measure in the incident response will be dictated by the organisation's incident response maturity; however the fundamental questions are:

- Was there a response at all to the alert?
- Who was alerted and was the alert escalated?
- What initial actions were taken?
- Did the message get back to the penetration tester?

SUMMARY

This chapter has discussed the importance of good penetration test coverage and what challenges may be faced in order to achieve it. The concept of test coverage necessarily touches upon topics strongly associated with scoping the test. Once that scope has been defined, it is important to get the penetration testing to achieve the coverage that is appropriate. While the commissioner of the test may not need to deal with the issues that can hamper good test coverage, it is vital that they recognise circumstances that may make it difficult to achieve, in order to be able to take any necessary action.

Similarly to test coverage, it is easy to fail to achieve the organisation's penetration testing requirements by inappropriately simulating the threat. This chapter also discussed some of the constraints applied to penetration tests and how they can be modified to reduce the impact on the threat simulation.

REFERENCES

Doctorow, C. (2004) Microsoft Research DRM talk. Available at: https://craphound.com/msftdrm.txt

Radichel, T. (2019) *Case Study: Critical Controls that Could Have Prevented Target Breach.* Bethesda, MD: SANS Institute. Available at: www.sans.org/reading-room/whitepapers/casestudies/case-study-critical-controls-prevented-target-breach-35412

Schneier, B. (2011) Schneier's Law. Schneier on Security, blog, 15 April 2011. Available at: https://www.schneier.com/blog/archives/2011/04/schneiers_law.html

Scholtz, T. and Heiser, J. (2013) ITScore for Information Security. Available at: https://www.gartner.com/doc/2507916/itscore-information-security

8 BUILDING ORGANISATIONAL CAPABILITY FOR PENETRATION TESTING

Ceri Charlton

This chapter discusses how organisations can go about developing the capacity to arrange to have penetration tests performed and the different ways in which this can be approached. In particular, it explores the relative strengths and weaknesses of performing this service with 'in-house' resources, using external resources or using a combination of both.

IN-HOUSE PENETRATION TESTING COMPARED WITH THIRD-PARTY PENETRATION TESTING

There are similarities and differences between 'in-house' and 'third-party' testing. In this section I elaborate on what exactly is meant by these terms.

'In-house' penetration testing is generally taken to mean that the penetration test has been performed by a direct employee of the organisation that owns the system or systems being tested. Although the exact nature will vary from organisation to organisation, the following list defines some of the key characteristics typical of such a role:

- Has experience of information security and, in particular, a good understanding of application and network vulnerabilities.

- Possesses a degree of organisational separation from the operational and development teams, who are involved in the delivery of the service being tested.

- Has access to toolkits and testing utilities, in order to identify vulnerabilities.

- Often has some form of formal certification or professional body membership, denoting a basic level of competence (and ideally, adherence to an ethical code) in the field of information security.

- Has communication skills in report writing and presentation, in order to provide a means of communicating findings of testing back to colleagues.

'Third-party' penetration testing on the other hand is typically understood to mean that the tests are conducted as a service, by another organisation – a 'service provider' – often on a per-test basis. Although the terms of such arrangements vary, the following list defines the key characteristics you can expect to encounter:

- This is typically performed **as a service** (similar to paid consultancy), rather than as a contract where the individual conducting the test might be employed indirectly to replace or supplement in-house staff.

- The individual conducting the test will usually specialise in testing the security of IT systems and often performs this activity as their core role. This degree of specialisation generally creates an expectation of a more comprehensive and up-to-date knowledge of testing tools and techniques.

- Based upon the needs of the client, the provider of the third-party penetration test (the individual(s) or the organisation responsible for conducting the test) will usually be required to hold a formal certification specific to penetration testing.

- The provision of reports should be highly professional and ideally have undergone some form of quality assurance, before being provided to the client.

- Typically, the third party will be less familiar with the system to be tested than an in-house tester would be; consequently, the accuracy of scoping is even more important to the success of the engagement.

Table 8.1 summarises at a high level some of the relative strengths and weaknesses of each approach. It should be noted that these are, by nature, generalisations. Not all organisations may exhibit all these tendencies, but they are generally recognisable as trends across industry as a whole at the time of writing. Even though the rise of software as a service (SaaS) will possibly reduce the amount of penetration testing needed for 'commodity IT' services such as email and file storage, it is highly likely that systems relating to the core function of non-IT businesses will continue to be developed in-house, for the business by an external developer, or consist of a third-party solution so heavily customised and configured as to warrant customer-specific penetration testing. This trend is likely to continue at least for the next decade.

Table 8.1 Comparison of penetration testing approaches

In-house penetration testing	External penetration testing
Advantages:	Advantages:
Focus on a single 'client' organisation	Larger 'teams' of testers allow for greater specialisation
Continuity of tester	
Greater integration with other teams/units	Greater cost transparency
	Economies of scale in 'tooling' time and cost
Flexibility of scheduling	
Understanding of broader business context	Demonstrably independent 'third-party' assurance
Trusted status allows modelling of 'insider threat'	

(Continued)

Table 8.1 (Continued)

In-house penetration testing	External penetration testing
Disadvantages:	Disadvantages:
Few organisations allow levels of focus necessary to operate as an expert	Timeboxing caused by commercial nature can lead to a rush
Harder to model an external attacker	Scoping tends to require more work to accurately define
May be accused of lacking impartiality	Ignorance of specific industry and associated data sensitivity can lead to oversights
	Lack of understanding of other systems inhibits 'bigger picture' view

The following sections elaborate on the general themes presented in Table 8.1.

Advantages of an in-house approach

In-house penetration testers do not suffer from the distraction of other clients, as they are able to focus solely on their own organisations' tests. This ability to focus is particularly valuable when performing re-tests: the actual action of performing a test may only take a few minutes.

A lot of the time spent performing a test is devoted to identifying where a vulnerability exists (for example, finding and recording it; identifying exactly where to perform the exploit) and, once discovered, the action can be performed again relatively quickly. In performing re-tests, usually, the more time that has elapsed, the longer it will take the individual performing the testing to pick up where they left off. In the case of in-house testers, they will have the advantage of continuity with a single 'client' (i.e. their own organisation) between tests and re-tests, so that they will typically be better placed to pick up where they left off, even after a period of time has passed since the last test.

The familiarity and continuity inherent in an internal tester can also be a benefit when performing subsequent tests of an application months, or even years, later. Recollection of earlier vulnerabilities can help not only in understanding **why** a given vulnerability exists (perhaps for the same underlying architectural reason it emerged previously), but in assisting staff involved in remediation activities. For example, it is a lot easier for an internal tester to help explain a Cross Site Scripting (XSS) vulnerability to a developer using language such as, 'Do you remember that problem we had two years ago in the search page of Application X? Well, we have just found that we have got the same thing on Application Y. Can you remember what you did to fix it on Application X?'

In comparison, an external tester will almost certainly need to rely on standardised, generic definitions of vulnerabilities, which, while convenient shorthand for information security professionals, may not be as easy to grasp for staff involved in remediation who lack good prior knowledge of information security. While time is typically set aside for a follow-up call, when this exceeds reasonable time constraints the commercial drivers of external penetration testers will typically result in a scope that merely communicates the findings. Testers will typically only engage in more detailed and time-consuming remediation coaching and training in the detail of the specific vulnerabilities as a separate engagement.

The existence of an internal penetration tester within the organisation can make for a smoother embedding of penetration testing as part of the broader lifecycle of systems being developed and deployed. It is generally much easier to (sometimes at short notice) schedule internal staff to perform a test or re-test, than wait for an external resource who may be booked up weeks in advance. Similarly, last-minute cancellations are relatively free in terms of financial penalties.

Aside from the lack of costs being incurred as a consequence of cancellation, there is also the risk of an organisation being tempted to make changes post-penetration test, and then releasing these (untested) changes into production if a test cannot be rescheduled. While this may still happen due to time pressures, the ability to reschedule internal personnel to perform a re-test without having to pay twice for a test reduces the likelihood of this situation arising.

If the scope of the penetration test is truly broad and permits the use of 'out of band'[1] or social engineering attacks, or seeks to test processes as well as applications, there are many ways in which the use of internal resources may be superior to the use of an external tester. These include:

- **Close and detailed knowledge of processes.** An employee who uses the organisation's processes day in, day out, will often have a knowledge of them that would take some external testers weeks to learn. This knowledge can be used to identify loopholes in a system which can be used to successfully socially engineer colleagues into unwittingly assisting the tester. For example, knowing both that a service desk will reset your password on your behalf and the location of staff availability calendars will allow for the impersonation of a staff member who is on annual leave, posing as them having returned 'early' from a holiday and having forgotten their password.

- **Knowledge of controls.** In much the same way as knowledge of processes can reveal 'holes' to be attacked, so too can knowledge of the controls that are in place allow an internal tester to evade detection in a way that might not be possible for an external tester. For example, if an internal employee is aware that before performing a password reset the service desk will always ring the desk phone of the named employee, it may occur to them to foil this control by putting a redirect from the desk phone to another phone which is in the possession of the tester.

- **Better 'big picture' view.** Internal testers are well placed to have a view not only of the specific system being tested, but also of the broader activities of the organisation and other systems. Whereas scoping, typically as a measure to constrain cost, tends to be very narrow with external testers, an internal tester cannot help but have some degree of awareness of the organisation outside the system currently under scrutiny. This broader view can, counter-intuitively, allow for a more focused test of a system, by reducing focus on attack vectors which are rendered somewhat irrelevant. For example, there is little interest in knowing that a WebDAV[2] vulnerability allows third parties to upload files to a web server if you are aware that another system run on the same infrastructure has the same permissions and offers this functionality. That is, the attack surface provided by the vulnerability is redundant in the sense that it already exists.

Combination of data from different sources

Elaborating on the concept of a better 'big picture' view, in-house penetration testers are often much better placed to identify risks arising from the combination of data from different sources.

Often, organisations hold data in multiple systems. Data from these disparate sources within the organisation, which may in isolation be harmless, can pose a threat when combined together. This is recognised as a specific and distinct threat.

As stated by the ICO:

> There is no doubt that non-recorded personal knowledge, in combination with anonymised data, can lead to identification.
>
> (ICO, 2012)

It is an increasingly recognised threat that two (or more) systems, which in isolation contain information which is lower risk, or even completely harmless or seemingly out-of-scope, become higher risk when combined. In relation to penetration testing specifically: (i) those involved in the arrangement of the tests should be mindful of this fact; and (ii) internal, rather than external, testers have the best chance of identifying such instances.

External testers, when working to a very specific scope (for example, only one of the systems is being tested), may not have any visibility of this particular threat at all – nor can they reasonably be expected to.

There have also been real-world Payment Card Industry, Data Security Standard (PCI DSS) breaches (i.e. theft of credit and debit card data) as a consequence of individuals within an organisation having access to two systems which masked[3] 16-digit card numbers in different ways, for example:

4659 1608 **** ****

**** **** 3848 2810

Testing either system in isolation would have appeared to offer a trivial risk and likely would not have attracted any comment. Yet, by identifying examples of the same record by comparing additional fields and meta-data, the two figures can be transposed together to produce a piece of sensitive information.

An external tester, by contrast, may be unaware of the existence of the other system within the environment, or may even have a very specific, narrow scope, which specifically excludes the other system and contractually binds them to focus on only one system. As a consequence, in almost all cases, an in-house tester will have a far greater visibility of such weaknesses within a system.

- **Tendency to be trusted**. Depending upon the size of the organisation, this effect can be extremely significant. While a service desk in a large multinational enterprise may be used to receiving calls from users whose name or voice they do not recognise, in smaller organisations it will not be. Similarly, an internal employee who works in the IT department, plugging a wireless access point into a switch is less likely to be challenged by colleagues in finance than an unrecognised third party in the office.

  This effect can also manifest itself particularly prominently when asking for information on processes or systems and requesting privilege escalations or violations of 'separation of duties'.

In many ways, an internal employee performing penetration testing can be thought of as the best simulation of an 'insider threat'; generally speaking, they are unlikely to be the most technically adept attackers, with knowledge of vulnerabilities that may be incomplete or out of date, but they can often make up for this in terms of their deep understanding of the organisation being targeted.

Disadvantages of an in-house approach

Although by no means applicable in every organisation, it is generally rare for internal employees to be given adequate time and resource to specialise in penetration testing alone. More frequently, in-house testers will be drawn from a pool of more general information security staff, or even from more general (i.e. non-security specific) 'testing' employees, with some interest or experience in information security. Only the very largest and most well-resourced security departments can afford the complete separation of operational security from internal personnel allocated to penetration testing.

Ironically, there is a tendency for organisations which **are** large enough to be in a position to justify employing dedicated in-house penetration testers to also be of such a size that many of the benefits of being in-house no longer apply. That is, such organisations are so large, with so many systems and processes, that it is generally unlikely that the internal tester performing a test on them will have the sort of intimate knowledge of them that makes internal testing beneficial.

Another factor that may render an in-house approach inappropriate is when an organisation specifically wants to perform black-box testing. An in-house tester, who must, by their very nature bring existing knowledge of the organisation and likely processes and systems, cannot reproduce this ignorance of the system.

Ultimately, senior risk owners must decide whether or not they require the additional assurance typically provided by third-party testers. Even where this is acceptable, in certain contexts, there can be requirements made by regulatory standards for the individuals and organisations that are permitted to perform penetration testing (e.g. the UK Government will often require CREST or CHECK certification as a condition of procuring penetration testing services).

For example, PCI DSS requires individuals assessing compliance to:

> Verify that the test was performed by a qualified internal resource or qualified external third-party and, if applicable, organizational independence of the tester exist...[4]

Looking to further drivers of behaviour and creating an environment that encourages the highest quality of internal penetration testing, there should be no negative consequences for the testers, such as having to be involved in the (typically unforecast) work of remediation. Ideally, to help enforce this separation of duties, in-house testers should have a separate reporting line from that of personnel responsible for remediation activities. Likewise, no objectives or targets should be selected for in-house testers (or their management) which may be jeopardised by delays to software releases caused by the result of the discovery of vulnerabilities.

Even when such measures are implemented, it is important to be cognisant that there can still be some degree of resentment, even pressure or hostility towards in-house testers from colleagues tasked with remediation. Even where this is not the case, there can be a **perception** from other interested parties (such as customers or regulators) that this pressure may compromise the integrity of the internal resource.

As a consequence of the above factors, in-house testers are generally considered to have a lower level of expertise in penetration testing as a discipline than third-party testers. This trend is likely to continue for the foreseeable future as technology stacks broaden and become more complex. This growing complexity of systems makes it harder to do penetration testing 'on the side' of other duties and, in fact, there is a general trend towards increasing specialisation and focus among even external testers who are able to focus full-time on the domain. That being said, in particularly well-resourced organisations, with high levels of maturity, in-house testers who are given the time, ability to focus and support are capable of operating at a level of effectiveness equivalent to, or even exceeding, that of external testers.

Advantages of third-party penetration testers

With the growing breadth of technologies used within IT, as a discipline in general, it is impossible to stay abreast of all developments, across all platforms, operating systems and technology stacks. In terms of penetration testing this can be even more true as the rate of publication of new vulnerabilities means that a high number are disclosed each week and it is beyond the reasonable capacity of one person to learn how to test for all of them.

Although in-house testers are not necessarily 'one-man bands', typically, they have fewer fellow security testers to pool knowledge with, and draw expertise from. Third parties, particularly in larger testing service providers, will have many colleagues, each with specialisations. This can provide a good opportunity for second opinions on more challenging tests, and also usually feeds into a useful quality assurance mechanism for sanity-checking reports.

This principle of specialisation is even more important when we consider more exotic, non-consumer IT systems, such as SCADA,[5] telephony and VOIP,[6] among others.

Inadequate testing, due to a lack of technical knowledge on the part of the tester may give a false sense of security. Where a given platform is sufficiently complex or unusual, experience of prior testing of it can be considerably easier to find (indeed, it can even be part of the selection process) when engaging with third-party testers.

Third-party testers also, by their nature, provide clear cost transparency for penetration testing, which needs to be factored in when making a decision about commissioning the development of new software. When third parties are used in this capacity, it also helps ensure that in-house testers are not distracted from their normal duties, and the direct cost inherent in utilising their time tends to help drive good quality focus on the most important systems being tested.

This directly apparent cost can also help drive efficiency. If internal staff are kept waiting, for example, when an environment is not yet ready, less commercially minded employees are usually more inclined to waste the internal testers' time than they would be with an external resource, charging a day-rate.

As with any service, there are also economies of scale to be realised by a full-time penetration tester. Setting up tooling for a penetration testing suite in particular and gaining familiarity with the means of trying a given vulnerability, in order to validate its existence within a system, are tasks which have a high initial cost in terms of set up time, but thereafter are quickly and easily reproducible. Even with report writing, an external tester will typically use templated text for repeatable report sections, such as the definition of a given vulnerability, to save time where creating this from scratch will provide little added-value. Given the specialisation of third-party testers, these costs of set up are only incurred once and the resulting charge to offset this can be spread across all their clients.

Disadvantages of third-party penetration testing suppliers

Skilled real attackers will often wait passively for significant periods of time (weeks or even months), performing passive observation known as 'recon' (reconnaissance), in order to gain knowledge of existing processes and controls and thus attain equivalent knowledge without revealing themselves. The commercial realities of an external tester mean that it is exceptionally unlikely that they will be given a large enough window of time, and to be paid commensurately, to be able to spend a realistic duration of 'recon' before beginning a penetration testing assignment.

To a certain extent, this can be mitigated by adopting a white-box testing approach (i.e. providing basic access and information to the tester in order to speed up this phase of the test). Nonetheless, it is often the case that if 'recon' were to be performed realistically, the tester would discover additional sources of information not necessarily provided in a white-box scenario. Examples would include:

- identifying details of dormant accounts;
- locating architectural diagrams in unsecured file shares;
- additional deployment documentation.

The commercial nature of third-party penetration tests mean that costs are typically calculated on a time (usually per-day) basis. A common problem, which manifests itself more commonly in third-parties' access to environments, is that their prerequisites are not in place at the time they are due to start. For example, network connectivity, details of a basic log-on, or even formal authorisation. To some degree, penetration testers factor in to their costs a certain amount of time to offset this delay. In reality, however, many clients still end up receiving considerably fewer hours' time in actual testing, particularly when they consider that a significant part of the time is also to be spent producing the resultant report.

Lack of knowledge of a customer's definition of sensitive information or market-specific compliance standards can, to some extent, be mitigated through good scoping and by briefing the third-party supplier on the specific fields of information to be targeted. Nonetheless, depending upon the complexity and breadth of the regulatory model in place (or just the diversity of seemingly innocuous data considered to be sensitive by the organisation being tested), it may not be reasonably possible to fully appraise the third-party tester of these.

When performing penetration testing of specialised systems, rather than traditional 'general purpose computing', non-industry-specific penetration testers may well be poorly qualified to perform tests on esoteric operating systems or hardware with which they are unfamiliar. As a trend, this is becoming less of an issue, as there is more of a convergence towards general purpose computing, and so while there is an ever-growing range of hardware on which software can run, there is also a growing degree of commonality between systems, such as the adoption of standardised protocols. For example, first- and second-generation SCADA control systems typically used proprietary hardware. It is only since the advent of third-generation SCADA control systems that they started to resemble more traditional network-connected computers, running (admittedly, 'hardened' or otherwise restricted) Linux/Unix derivatives on a network more akin to a traditional TCP/IP network.[7] Arguably, on older first- and second-generation SCADA systems (and in other similar proprietary or specialised applications) a typical penetration tester, from a more general background, will lack the expertise to perform a meaningful penetration test.

Older, more hardware-based information systems (for example, those that resemble circuit boards or telephony platforms more than a 'computer' in the standard sense) often have few 'fixes' available for their vulnerabilities. Nonetheless, where appropriate penetration testing of such systems can be performed, despite this lack of available remediation, they can still provide useful information. Discovering multiple vulnerabilities in a legacy SCADA system that is hardware-constrained to use insecure protocols, for example, is still useful intelligence from an IT security perspective. Knowing that these vulnerabilities exist:

- Allows risks associated to be raised through an organisation's risk management process (it is generally acknowledged that just because a risk can't be 'treated', it is not a reason not to track the risk).

- Where such risks are identified, it might be possible to mitigate the risks elsewhere, or through other means. For example, the use of no-longer-secure encryption protocols can be managed to some extent by restricting access to the network over which they run.

- Even where such risks are wholly untreatable, knowing about their quantity and severity can help make a case to secure funding to replace the system with newer, more readily 'fixable' systems. This can in fact be one of the times when information security can be seen as a boon, as such risks can lend weight to operational colleagues' requests to fund replacements for aged systems.

These advantages of performing meaningful penetration testing and analysis mean that even in the context of systems where no fixes are available, good quality penetration testing, by testers with knowledge of this specific technology and its context, can still bring value. Therefore, organisations ought to consider whether this assurance can be best fulfilled by an external penetration tester, especially if this tester does not demonstrably possess this technology-specific expertise, where perhaps an available in-house resource does.

Although the majority of penetration testers are competent, ethical and attempt to deliver a good quality test and report, unlike many other forms of work, or even forms of testing, the nature of penetration testing creates a peculiarity that 'high quality and principled' is not always seen as a good value by prospective customers. If the motive of all customers were genuinely to have a penetration tester discover as many weaknesses as possible, common sense would apply, and the 'best' penetration testers would be most commercially successful. A good quality penetration tester, however, may find that, counter-intuitively, their thorough test that discovers twice as many vulnerabilities as their competition is resented. Furthermore, their refusal to downplay the severity of a vulnerability in (or even to omit entirely from) their report at the client's request can also engender hostility.

This can manifest itself particularly under regulatory or compliance frameworks that require that penetration testing occurs, but which do not adequately enforce quality, or even certify penetration testing organisations to their standards. In such environments, rather than being the willing purchaser of what amounts to assurance services, a customer may only really be looking to buy a report that can be presented to a regulator or auditor, as evidence that no high or critical vulnerabilities exist, and that this state has been verified by an allegedly competent and honest third party.

Under such a set of circumstances, each additional finding, coupled with a refusal to leave it out of the report, is another item to be fixed for the client who may really rather have just had a cleaner report. Clearly, in such a model, the less competent the tester, the fewer vulnerabilities found and therefore, the more desirable in the eyes of the client. While such an approach may not even occur to a responsible, well-intentioned organisation which genuinely wants to discover its vulnerabilities, it should be borne in mind when selecting penetration testing vendors and goes some way to explaining the continued survival in the marketplace of certain less competent vendors.

HYBRID APPROACHES

In many ways, almost all third-party tests, other than a black-box test, involve some degree of assistance being provided to the third party in the form of knowledge about the system or systems to be tested and answers to queries, among others. Usually, however, these are constrained to answering questions necessary to facilitate the performance of the test, rather than internal and third-party testers working together. In this section, we discuss some options which further blur this distinction.

Early SDLC internal testing combined with end-of-cycle third-party tests

In software development lifecycle (SDLC) cost models, it is widely recognised that the earlier in the lifecycle a defect (security or otherwise) is found, the cheaper and simpler the remediation is. Although this relative cost is decreasing, in part due to increasing adoption of Agile and DevOps methodologies,[8] it is still preferable to perform remediation earlier on in the SDLC, to ensure that security is 'built-in' as opposed to being retrofitted.

Figure 8.1 'Cost to fix'

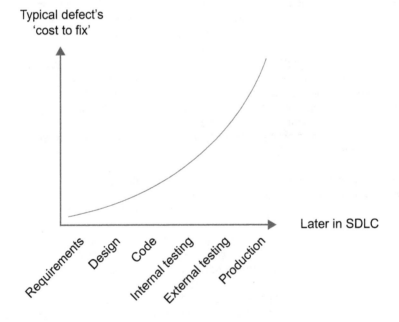

Although generic and stylised, Figure 8.1 shows the way that this concept is also typically represented in relation to any change being made to address a defect (security or otherwise). Essentially, any steps preceding the point in the SDLC process before a defect is detected are sunk costs in terms of resources and effort expended.

The more of these steps that occur before discovery, the greater the wasted effort and hence the more significant the cost of remediation. This creates desirability to detect defects as early as possible; you sometimes hear this referred to as 'moving security left in the SDLC' or, even more confusingly, 'getting security to the left'.

For this reason, one form of hybrid approach is to perform at least some security testing earlier in the development lifecycle, in addition to third-party penetration testing. The intent being to at least **reduce** the number of vulnerabilities detected at the (later) third-party penetration testing stage.

The topic of what exactly constitutes a penetration test is almost a whole discussion in itself (see Chapter 1). It is generally accepted that penetration testers will make use of automated testing tools to some extent as part of the test. At the same time, few informed testers would claim that running a fully automated test alone was an acceptable penetration test.

It may well be beyond the ability of the internal resource to be able to test for the same breadth of vulnerabilities as a dedicated third-party specialist, but tests they can perform bring some benefit. For example, as a starting point when developing this capability, it may be appropriate to identify and formalise a small number of specific, commonly occurring vulnerabilities to be tested for in the earlier, internal test, for example, those in the OWASP[9] Top 10.

Even if the third party were to subsequently find additional vulnerabilities, every vulnerability that is found earlier improves things. Specifically, by:

- being able to reach a 'go live' or 'no go live' decision sooner;
- giving more time before scheduled release dates to remediate the identified vulnerability;
- reducing the quantity of re-testing that needs to be performed by an external penetration tester.

Over time, if the internal testing is implemented to a high enough standard and is broad enough in its scope, this model can provide a very good quality means of testing. Under such a format, the third-party penetration test's purpose is primarily a 'backstop' to processes which should have already caught vulnerabilities and also provide the formality of a review by a fully independent third party. Such an approach can be viewed as analogous to the way in which organisations tend to make use of an audit structure consisting of both internal and external resources. The hope is that the internal audit will have the ongoing and more detailed view, due to a constant presence, whereas the external audit often has greater technical capabilities and their involvement helps demonstrate that there is little scope for impropriety.

Internal re-testing capability

As a result of any penetration test, there is usually an expectation that there will be some form of remediation performed, followed by a re-test to validate whether the remediation has been successful.

A high-level flow diagram outlining this is shown in Figure 8.2.

In most commercial engagements, third parties will either charge for re-testing or, at the very least, be careful to include a contractual caveat which ensures that only a certain amount of time will be allocated to re-testing, or that any given re-test will only

---

Figure 8.2 Typical workflow of penetration testing and remediation

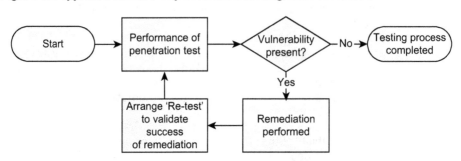

be performed once. Without such provisions, a third-party tester would be exposed to a requirement to perform significant amounts of additional work.

This could easily become unsustainable if, for example, the organisation being tested was repeatedly unsuccessful in its attempt to remediate a given vulnerability; or if due to poorly architected software[10] the same vulnerability exists as distinct occurrences across many hundreds of pages or forms, each of which would need to be re-tested.

Therefore, one useful capability which can be developed in-house is the ability to perform re-tests of vulnerabilities that have been **previously identified** by third-party testers. Rather than trying to maintain an encyclopaedic knowledge of techniques which are changing on an almost daily basis, the focus can shift to developing the capability to be able to learn a specific vulnerability that has been identified and how to recreate that one exploit.

Advantages of such an approach include:

- Having the capability to, at very short notice, perform a re-test...

- ...As a consequence of this, being able to condense the 'remediate, re-test, release' cycle.

- Ability to spend time with developers and deployment personnel in order to teach them how to validate that the fix has worked. Where a specific vulnerability exists in multiple locations within a system, this can be particularly valuable. Conversely, external penetration testers are not likely to have the time (or inclination) to effectively train others how to do their job, thereby reducing the demand for their own services, unless this is pursued as a separate chargeable task.

- Possibility to integrate testing for the specific vulnerability identified, into automated vulnerability detection occurring earlier in the SDLC.

The bar of such a form of in-house testing is considerably lower than that of being able to conduct a full penetration test in which it is necessary to first discover the existence of vulnerabilities within a system (and equally importantly, be comfortable that the test has identified the majority of disclosed vulnerabilities that are present). It is therefore a capability which can be developed more readily. Automated tools such as Metasploit[11] often have the ability to perform specific tests and run limited scope tests for identified vulnerabilities using 'packages' specific to a given vulnerability. Provided a package is available for the specific vulnerability, the process to execute the test differs little from vulnerability to vulnerability. Often, it requires very little understanding of the underlying vulnerability in order to perform it.

One of the disadvantages of solely relying on automated tools is that you are dependent upon waiting for a 'package' containing a given exploit before you can perform the test. Even where automated tools are used for convenience, speed and automated testing,[12] in order to be able to test for a vulnerability straight away it is often necessary to develop manual testing capabilities. Slower SDLC cycles, however, are less affected by this, as by their very nature re-tests usually occur at least a few days after the vulnerability was detected. Therefore, even for recently disclosed vulnerabilities, by the time it comes to re-testing the relevant package the automated tool has often become available.

Collaborative penetration testing

Although very rarely seen in practice, one particularly powerful form of testing can be to get the best of both approaches, by allocating an in-house tester (or at least an internal employee with the knowledge of the organisation, system and its processes) to work with a third-party tester.

Although not yet a recognised term, I would propose the term, 'collaborative penetration testing' to describe such an approach. In many ways this could be seen as an extension to white-box testing in that you will be providing a skilled external tester with all the 'insider knowledge' of an in-house tester. The theory behind such an approach is that you can seek to get the best of both in-house and third-party approaches.

In terms of modelling a 'real-world threat', such an approach would be analogous to an insider – perhaps not even in IT, much less in information security – who has knowledge of the organisation's processes and systems working in conjunction with a more technically capable outsider who can provide the knowledge to guide and direct a malicious hack. Such an attack may appear far-fetched, but it is worth noting that it is not unheard of (for example Buchanan, 2006; Bryars, 2015): in multiple cases, UK police have verified that criminal gangs have coerced or blackmailed internal personnel into 'assisting' in this manner. So, it is possible that structuring a penetration test in this way is a more meaningful strategy than it may first appear.

SUMMARY

In conclusion, there are merits to both in-house and external penetration testing and there is no reason that the different approaches should be viewed as mutually exclusive, as opposed to complementary, measures. The chapter has discussed how, as systems' release cycles become more frequent, it is becoming more necessary to use approaches that blend both automated testing and testing performed by human testers. Some reasons why it is increasingly desirable to perform at least some security testing earlier in the software lifecycle have also been presented.

REFERENCES

Bryars, M. (2015) Securing the contact centre from the inside out. *SC Magazine*, 26 May 2015. Available at: https://www.scmagazineuk.com/securing-contact-centre-inside/article/1478733

Buchanan, R. (2006) Call centres infiltrated by gangs. *BBC News*, 26 October 2006. Available at: http://news.bbc.co.uk/1/hi/scotland/glasgow_and_west/6089736.stm

Information Commissioner's Office (2012) *Anonymisation: Managing Data Protection Risk Code of Practice*. Wilmslow, UK: ICO. Available at: https://ico.org.uk/media/1061/anonymisation-code.pdf

9 COMMISSIONING PENETRATION TESTS

Peter Taylor

Penetration testing has been a standard security control for more than a decade, and has become, to an extent, a 'routine' requirement for organisations that require evidence of testing to comply with their regulatory or industry sector standards (the payment card industry PCI DSS standard for example). In response to this, a wide range of penetration test service providers has emerged within the information security marketplace. Some of these focus very closely on vulnerability and security testing, while others include test capability as one of many offerings within their portfolio.

Findings from a research project conducted by Jerakano Limited on behalf of CREST in 2016–17 (Creasey and Glover, 2017) indicated that the top three reasons why organisations hire external third-party suppliers are because these suppliers can:

1. Provide more experienced, dedicated technical staff who understand how to carry out penetration tests effectively.

2. Perform an independent assessment of their security arrangements.

3. Carry out a full range of testing (for example, black-, white- or grey-box; internal or external; infrastructure or web application; source code review; and social engineering).

Other reasons given for using external suppliers are because they can:

- Deploy a structured process and plan, developed by experts.

- Increase the scope and frequency of tests.

- Conduct short-term engagements, eliminating the need to employ your own specialised (and often expensive) staff – and reducing the cost of training (and re-training) internal teams.

- Take advantage of automation (for example, penetration testing workflows, importing vulnerability management reports).

AN OVERVIEW OF THE PENETRATION TESTING SERVICE PROVIDER MARKET

The security testing marketplace includes a spectrum of capability in terms of test quality and depth. At the simplest level, some organisations specialise in providing standard commoditised test suites, based on tools and 'scanning' technology. These provide a relatively low-cost and low-overhead (in terms of business support) test scope.

Standardised testing can establish that systems are secure against common and widely encountered security threats. This level of testing can be fully adequate for a small- or medium-sized organisation with relatively simple or small-scale IT systems. This is the level of testing typically commissioned in support of accreditation to a standard security level, such as the Cyber Essentials Plus Scheme.[1] It is even possible for some organisations to undertake standard tests of this type themselves using licensed tools, either in-house or from a cloud-based testing service. That said, where sensitive or high-value assets are to be assured a more informed and in-depth test approach would always be recommended.

More complex testing capability can include provision of a wider range of tools, particularly where a more high-end IT application set is in use. Organisations that have internet-facing applications with a wide range of user interaction, or in particular, supporting financial transactions, would normally opt to go beyond the level of 'standard' tests and incorporate more individual tester expertise. This requires more capability from the testing provider, and usually more input from the commissioning organisation on the nature of their applications, how they operate and what functions exhibit the most risk.

Going further, some organisations – particularly those in financial or market-sensitive sectors – may want a very deep and thorough assessment of their security risk profile. This can extend beyond simple penetration testing and into 'Red Team'-style testing, where testers use expertise, guile and techniques such as profiling of their target and social engineering to develop a sophisticated threat 'package' which is used in an attempt to circumvent installed security controls.

TEST PROVIDER CAPABILITIES

At one time, security testing was as simple as running through a set of standard tests and checks against a system – looking for user accounts that do not require a password for access, looking for open access folders or web servers, looking for services that respond to queries or commands without requiring credentials, and so forth. In a way, penetration testing still follows a similar cycle; but the scope of the vulnerabilities and bugs to be assessed has grown exponentially with the combinations of system types, applications, services and interfaces that information systems have.

Identifying an appropriate testing partner to help you to understand security risks requires some awareness of the scale of this problem and an ability to converse with and assess the offerings and capabilities of potential testers. The ideal test provider will have an awareness of information technologies that is both wide and deep. They will also have some experience and familiarity with standards and applications used in your business sector.

They should be able to reference and use a range of testing tools and techniques to interrogate your systems, as well as adopt recognised methodologies for testing and know how to apply these. But, of course, they must also be able to express their findings from the use of these tools and techniques at a level that is clear and useful to your organisation.

A starting point for selecting test providers is their accreditation. In the UK, and increasingly internationally, the recognised source for establishing the credentials of cyber-security advisors is CREST.[2] In assessing providers for accreditation CREST reviews the skill and competency, methodology, quality controls and trust credentials (for example, through staff background checks) of cyber-security suppliers and service providers. The CREST system initially complemented, and has now largely succeeded, other accreditation initiatives such as the UK CESG CHECK scheme that applied similar criteria to assess the capability of security testing providers.

However, there are other accreditations to look for from reputable providers, and these may be useful in differentiating between potential offerings. Relevant assurance can be gained from certification to recognised security standards. In the UK the Cyber Essentials Plus scheme is gaining increased relevance, as is the ISO27001 standard internationally. Another area that can be assessed is the level of qualification held by key staff of a testing provider and their membership of appropriate professional bodies.

A range of qualifications are aimed directly at evidencing penetration testing capability. The most widely recognised are probably the GPEN qualification issued by GIAC or the OSCP from Offensive Security but there are also certifications issued by CREST, the CEH (Certified Ethical Hacker) or CPT (Certified Penetration Tester) qualifications. Broader information security professional qualifications, for example, the ISC2 CISSP[3] or ISACA CISM[4] and CISA qualifications, evidence a good level of competence to advise and investigate security capability.

An additional factor that can be used to indicate tester capability is the profile and experience of their team. Most security testing companies will provide prospective clients with an overview of their management and technical team covering qualifications, experience and expertise. Look for a wide range of experience and mix of competence. Good security testing requires contemporary and practised technical competence, but also a wider background in problem solving, planning, and even psychology and social engineering. A capable test provider will be able to offer you a good mix of experience, depth and technical currency.

WORKING RELATIONSHIPS WITH TESTERS

Any arrangement to perform security testing must be founded on both a sound formal contractual basis, and on a clear level of understanding between the client and the testers about the objectives and scope of the testing. Negotiating a contract for penetration tests is to some extent similar to other types of contract negotiation in business and IT. Many contracts are based on standard terms and conditions which set out the parameters within which both the testing team and the organisation being tested will operate.

Confidentiality is a prime consideration. In order to test effectively, testing providers require access to information about their client's systems, networks and business structure. They may also need to share information with their client in order to make tests practical, such as network (IP) addresses or test system credentials. This creates a need for a mutual understanding and agreement on confidentiality around test information that must be observed by all stakeholders and participants. At the simplest level, this might be a non-disclosure agreement but there may also be a need to segregate access to information in order to make tests meaningful, particularly if these are more complex and multi-environment tests.

One of the biggest challenges for penetration testers is where systems are co-hosted in multi-tenanted environments, and where tests against one hosted application might have an impact on a separate system or system owner. There may also be some requirements around disclosure of test results; for example, where a system hosted by one supplier is being tested independently by another. Testing agreements should be clear and unambiguous about what party owns and is responsible for the dissemination of any test results and how these can be used.

Testing may involve access to personal data, in which case both the test client and testers must handle that data in accordance with privacy law. An example where this can come into play is where testing teams are located outside of the geographic area of the data hosting source, for example outside the EU, or they use testing tools hosted outside the EU. In that case, contracts must ensure that security and privacy of any personal data accessed during a test will be preserved in accordance with the General Data Protection Regulation (GDPR).

Where applicable, handling of personal data should be addressed in the contract with penetration testers. In light of GDPR this is particularly important where international boundaries are a factor in testing. While it is not within the scope of this chapter to cover GDPR in detail, testing providers will be aware of their privacy obligations and should recognise the need to clarify these contractually. The data privacy regulators (the ICO in the UK) provide guidance on contractual provisions regarding data protection and these should be adopted for testing that may impact individual privacy.[5]

REVIEW AND 'ROTATION' OF TEST PROVIDERS

A control that is often recommended for penetration testing is that organisations 'rotate' their testing provision between different providers over a rolling period. This can range from an arrangement in which several potential test providers are retained and offered the chance to 'bid' for specific test contracts as they arise (which can clearly offer commercial benefits), through to a periodic re-tender and re-contract for a longer lasting 'exclusive' test contract.

There are benefits in both building and maintaining a strong relationship with a trusted test service provider and in having a range of options. A test provider that has tested a client's systems several times can build up a good understanding of their technical and organisational environment. This can lead to an improvement in the quality of the testing over time. It may also be easier to secure consent for tests by a known and trusted provider that has worked with your IT services or peer group companies previously.

Conversely, test strategies should take into account the dynamic nature of cyber threats. The risk environment changes frequently, and test techniques and capabilities evolve in line with this. A good test service provider should be aware of and respond to this, proactively reviewing their approach with you on a regular basis. If not, you should consider seeking alternative proposals for testing periodically to evaluate them against incumbent service providers. It can also be useful to consider specialist organisations with particular skills where you require a test of a new or 'niche' technology that might fall outside the skillset of previous test providers.

TEST CONSENTS

Consent for testing is rarely a bilateral issue between penetration tester and the client. It is not unusual for one or two separate layers of client service providers to be party to testing, and their awareness and consent to tests can be essential. For example, in testing a web-hosted application it is possible that one service provider is responsible primarily for providing the application and its functionality while another (possibly a cloud service provider) is responsible for the hosting.

Separate stakeholders will be subject to service liabilities, security controls of their own and contractual requirements, surrounding security tests. It is standard practice to seek consent from such service providers as a prerequisite of commissioning a penetration test. It can also be useful to engage with them to ensure that testing activity might not be misinterpreted and 'reacted to' inappropriately. For example, many hosting providers adopt overarching security controls which interpret a security scan as hostile activity and might block or redirect network traffic generated by the test process.

This is increasingly the case for cloud-hosted services where integral security controls are provided inside the cloud platform. Cloud service contracts generally require that clients request permission from the provider before conducting penetration testing of any part of their environment. Note that in some cases, standard security controls may have to be 'relaxed' to permit testing to take place at all. Because of this, most hosting providers will now have a standard approach to evaluation of and consenting to independent security tests. Engagement with this process should be a standard component of any penetration test plan.

Organisations that make extensive use of cloud services should study the assurance issued by their hosting provider and assess how penetration testing activity might complement this. It can be useful to review some of the developing standards and checklists for cloud security, for example those issued by the National Cyber Security Centre (NCSC)[6] or the Cloud Security Alliance.[7] You should also allow for some detailed discussions with your testing provider around the nature and scope of tests directed at cloud-hosted services.

COMMERCIAL AND TECHNICAL RELATIONSHIPS

Fees for performing penetration testing are obviously central to the contracting process. The actual cost of a test can vary significantly among test providers, business sectors and technical environments. It is always worth conducting initial surveys of potential suppliers through a 'request for proposals' (RFP) process prior to entering into a full negotiation, to gain an understanding of the potential costs.

Typical contents of a penetration testing RFP

High-level business objectives of conducting the test, for example:

- Is this testing for insurance purposes?
- Are the tests to confirm assurances from a service provider?
- Are you subject to regulatory or contractual requirements for the tests?

High-level scope of the testing, in terms of services, sites or servers to be included.

An overview of the technical architecture of the services to be tested (though not necessarily full technical details at the RFP stage).

The time frame within which you would ideally want the testing completed, including any timing constraints such as dates (year or month end periods to be avoided, requirements for testing to be conducted out of business hours).

Key contacts and communication protocols for further information – secure email, file transfer options.

Like all service markets, the security consultancy and testing business is subject to the rules of supply and demand. It is well known that good security skills are in short supply, and test service providers can sometimes charge a premium. Flexibility in scheduling can have a significant impact. If you set out to engage a large and complex penetration test programme to a short deadline with fixed delivery dates, you may find it hard to secure resource at a reasonable cost. Alternatively, if you engage a service provider well in advance, and plan for a series of test engagements with a flexible timetable over a long period, you could negotiate a very favourable deal overall for the cost of your test programme.

Be aware of the difference between skilled and in-depth security testing and standard technical or security consultancy. While technical support is normally charged at an hourly rate, elapsed time consumed by a penetration test does not necessarily bear much relationship to the total effort or cost required for it to be completed.

Penetration testing may involve long periods of automated assessment and scanning of networks and applications, interspersed with short, but intensive, periods of manual analysis to interpret results. In fact, the most valuable element of any testing engagement is the analysis and interpretation phase in which a range of findings, vulnerabilities and test logs are translated into a coherent picture of the risk profile of the test target. This may require more than one technical discipline – and hence imply collaboration between one or more testing specialists – adding to the complexity and cost of test analysis.

Test results have to be delivered in a usable format. Software tool-driven tests can produce copious amounts of technical information and test logs that could be unintelligible to a non-expert reviewer. The time taken to collate this into a presentable report is part of the cost of testing, as also is some additional time for the material to be reviewed and quality assessed for completeness. Good test providers tend to combine communication and documentation skills with their wider technical skill base, in order to provide high-quality reporting.

UNDERSTANDING AND USING TEST RESULTS

An important element of the relationship between a test provider and their client is the understanding that the penetration testers have of their client's requirements and expectations from the test. Clients usually have some specific outputs they would like to see from test results, ranging from a 'clean bill of health' for their systems, through to a risk-based prioritisation of areas in which they should focus their defensive security investment and effort.

It is rare that penetration tests are conducted purely as a discovery exercise in which a client wants a full disclosure of all risks that can be identified, from the most critical down to the trivial. Testing engagements should seek clarity as to the level of reporting that is required by the client and what their appetite is for detail and risk level to be reported. When engaging penetration test providers, always ask to review sample reports (anonymised and desensitised, as appropriate) to gain an understanding up front of the type of material that will be issued at the end of the test. Ideally testing providers should be prepared to talk their clients through the results of these examples to clarify their meaning.

Penetration test service provider companies use standard vulnerability classification schemes that have a direct meaning to their clients in terms of risk levels. The most 'common currency' of vulnerability tends to be the categories used by Microsoft for classifying their software security updates. These range from low through moderate and important to critical levels of risk. In some environments, however, more sophisticated scoring and assessment models can be required (particularly IT infrastructure and service provider networks). A widely used example that some testing providers adopt is the Software Engineering Institute's OCTAVE[8] methodology, which measures both the impact of a particular vulnerability and the likelihood that it might be exploited in a particular organisational context.

Experienced testing providers will also be able to articulate their findings in relation to other models and methodologies. A commonly used reference is the OWASP Application Security Verification Standard[9] project which sets out to analyse and categorise common risks to web applications. Another is the Cloud Security Alliance (2012)[10] guidance on web application security assessments.

Ideally penetration test results should provide more than a simple list of risks and vulnerabilities. A capable test provider may be able to outline not just the vulnerability, but also what the outcome of it being exploited might mean for a given organisation. This could be in terms of service disruption, data loss or theft, or financial impact.

A good test report may also provide advice regarding remediation of vulnerabilities and provide references to sources of data, software or hardware updates or vendor recommendations for configuration to address test findings.

SUMMARY

This chapter has considered the market for penetration testing service provision and drawn attention to the varied services that are available. It has looked at a number of different types of testing and suggested approaches to selecting them in line with business requirements.

We have looked at some of the contractual and commercial factors that arise in penetration testing engagements. This has also included consideration of a range of certification and qualification regimes that can be used to gain assurance about potential test providers.

We have also looked at some of the processes that testing engagements will typically follow, including eliciting proposals, setting up agreements and contracting for provision of results. Finally we looked at the interpretation of test results and ways of gaining the optimal value from them.

REFERENCES

Cloud Security Alliance (2012) *SecaaS Implementation Guidance: Category 5 // Security Assessments*. Available at: https://downloads.cloudsecurityalliance.org/initiatives/secaas/SecaaS_Cat_5_Security_Assessments_Implementation_Guidance.pdf

Creasey, J. and Glover, I. (2017) *A Guide for Running an Effective Penetration Testing Programme*. CREST. Available at: https://crest-approved.org/wp-content/uploads/CREST-Penetration-Testing-Guide.pdf

10 SELECTING TOOLS FOR PENETRATION TESTING

Jims Marchang and Roderick Douglas

Organisations that contract specialist penetration testing services need not necessarily be concerned about which tools and techniques may be used to test their systems, as they are mainly interested in the test results. However, some knowledge of the tools and techniques used in penetration testing will assist managers in developing an awareness of threats and vulnerabilities, and will help them define an appropriate scope for the tests.

CONTEXT

There are organisations that publish guidelines on penetration test programmes. CREST, a not-for-profit organisation that offers assurance of processes and procedures for the technical information security industry, suggests a nine-step testing phase (CREST, 2017), while the Penetration Testing Execution Standard (PTES, 2017) defines seven main sections, and SANS defines five or six, dependent on whether 'Cleaning Up' should be included (Wai, 2002). The agreed scope of a penetration test will determine which stages are appropriate.

The type of penetration test undertaken should determine the amount of planning, co-ordination and communication between the testers and the client. In some cases, the client will have no knowledge of where, when or how the testers will operate, and no co-ordination is required. In other cases, activities will be restricted to a specific time and location, with a limited scope. Where penetration tests are conducted during normal business operations, specific activities may need to be excluded. Some tests may disrupt production services: for example large amounts of traffic from penetration probing on a network which is already saturated with organisational traffic could lead to a degradation of the network performance. Some systems are vulnerable to attacks which can cause them to fail. Penetration testing at critical or busy times for organisations should be avoided, unless this is the specific focus of the test.

It should also be emphasised that penetration testing without proper authority is a contravention of the Computer Misuse Act (Daintith and Wright, 2008). Organisations and testers should ensure that full legal authority is given to the penetration testers for the activities they are requested to undertake.

In some cases, a genuine attack may take place at the time a penetration test is under way. If the penetration tester discovers this, they should immediately notify the organisational incident response team.

If the penetration testing uncovers evidence of prior penetration, such as backdoor accounts or ports open, then this information should also be passed to the appropriate team. Once a penetration test is under way, there should be a clear authority with the right to stop or change the test. This will avoid the situation where IT staff may attempt to influence the activities of a tester in order to avoid the exposure of vulnerabilities for which they will be held responsible. However, there may be genuine reasons to modify a test once under way, and the decision-making process should be clear before testing begins.

When selecting and agreeing tools for a penetration test, care should be taken over the integrity of all tools used. Whether downloaded from public internet sites or directly obtained from suppliers, tools must verified as identical to the originals as published by the creator, otherwise it is possible that the tools themselves could contain malicious code which deliberately introduces vulnerabilities for later exploitation. Storms (2006) suggests a number of ways of doing this including cryptographic hashes and digital signatures. Assuring the integrity and authenticity of penetration testing tools is particularly important as penetration testers are often given access to privileged or secure areas of a system.

A cryptographic hash check involves calculating the cryptographic hash of the digital information in question according to a well-known mathematical formula such as SHA-256 or MD5. The result of this calculation is a large number which can be considered the digital fingerprint of the information. The calculated number is compared with the known and published cryptographic hash of the original data. If the two numbers are different it can be concluded that the information has been modified and is not identical to the original.

Furthermore, some penetration testing techniques could involve the deliberate uploading of components to live servers, or modification of settings to enable particular exploits. Such procedures must be approved in advance, and any modifications made must be undone after the testing.

ASSESSING THE MOST APPROPRIATE PENETRATION TESTING TOOLS AND TECHNIQUES FOR THE PROGRAMME

Penetration test service providers will often have a specific suite of tools which their penetration testers are required to use.

In this section, the terms 'tools' and 'techniques' are considered synonymous, as most tools are designed to facilitate a particular technique of penetration testing.

However, some organisations may choose to conduct in-house tests and they will have a range of tools from which to choose. A combination of different tools can be used where each tool is specialised in operating in one or more of the penetration testing phases, for example, those defined by Chiem and Yan (2014): reconnaissance; enumeration; exploitation.

Some penetration test tools are free or open-source, and some proprietary. Proprietary tools may come in several versions, with free trial versions limited in some way such as update availability, number of targets to scan or operational time. While free or open-source tools may avoid initial purchase costs, they sometimes require a higher level of expertise to use or maintain.

Penetration test tools may also be available as frameworks rather than specific tools. These frameworks allow different combinations of exploits, payloads, delivery vectors and encoding mechanisms to be used to assemble a specialised attack tool. Such frameworks allow modules or add-ons to be written and incorporated as new vulnerabilities are discovered (Faircloth, 2016).

Penetration testers may also choose to build a complete operating system environment with all the tools installed and available to use. Such a system may be installed directly on hardware, but is more often deployed as a virtual machine (VM) on a laptop computer. Having a separate penetration testing VM on a laptop will allow a penetration tester to take their complete suite of testing tools into the testing environment, while still allowing their device to be used for normal computing requirements at other times.

The most widely used penetration testing environment is the Kali Linux distribution (Allen et al., 2014), which is preconfigured with a wide variety of penetration testing tools.

Reconnaissance tools

If the penetration test is of the black-box type, where little or no information is given to the tester about the internal structure of the network and target systems, then several open-source intelligence (OSINT) tools may be helpful before the actual penetration test begins. These tools will range from straightforward search engines to comprehensive applications that investigate DNS and IP records, social media and blogs. The goal of this early investigation is to find out as much as possible about an organisation, its structure, buildings, staff, systems and networks to determine which attacks are most likely to succeed.

If the penetration test is of the white-box type, where the internal structure of the network and systems, or even the hosts and applications are known to the tester, then such tools are not needed, and the target hosts or networks can be investigated directly.

If the scope of the penetration test is not limited to a fixed set of systems, then one of the first tasks may be to find hosts, services, applications and ports available as potential targets. The tool of choice for this is Nmap (Kaur and Kaur, 2017). Nmap is a powerful scanning tool which can be used in different ways, from sending simple ICMP echo requests to a range of IP addresses, to 'host fingerprinting', which is attempted by crafting specialised TCP/IP packets which are outside of the normal range encountered (for example, having SYN(chronise), ACK(nowledgement) and RST (reset) flags all set), and using the responses obtained to determine information about the target.

Different operating systems or protocol stacks generally respond differently to such unusual packets, enabling fingerprinting of the system. In addition, Nmap has an in-built scripting language which allows development of scripts to control its behaviour. Other tools among many in this category, also included in the Kali Linux distribution, are Sparta, a scanning and enumeration tool; p0f, an operating system fingerprinting tool; and snmp-check, a tool which can retrieve detailed host information using the SNMP protocol.

Enumeration tools

Once IP addresses, protocols and ports have been identified, a penetration tester can move to more detailed vulnerability assessment tools. At this point, a penetration tester needs to be able to identify particular vulnerabilities that may be used to gain access to systems. CVE (common vulnerabilities and exposures) lists are lists of known vulnerabilities in systems (Mell and Grance, 2002).

Organisations supplying and maintaining software code, including both open-source and proprietary systems, need to update their software with security patches for any discovered vulnerabilities, and will maintain public lists of vulnerabilities and patches. Many such lists exist, and CVE is a centralised list of known exposures from more than 150 organisations covering over 300 products, described by Tripathi and Singh (2010, p. 382) as 'a universally accepted dictionary of common vulnerabilities and exposures'. It is useful for penetration testers to be able to relate the results of their tests to items in the CVE list. Several vulnerability scanners offer this capability.

Nessus is a widely used tool for testing potential vulnerabilities. Although the application is sometimes described as 'open-source', a key must be purchased from its vendor Tenable in order to download the latest plug-ins. Nessus developers constantly monitor CVE lists and develop plug-ins that enable Nessus to identify the latest vulnerabilities, test for their presence on target systems, give an indication of the severity of the problem and suggest remediation.

A number of other vulnerability scanners are available which perform this function. Some are integrated into wider 'Vulnerability Management' solutions. Other notable tools of this nature are available from BeyondTrust, Qualys, Rapid7 and Tripwire (Barros and Chuvakin, 2015; Holm, 2012). Given a list of hosts and ports to test, these tools will generally perform an automated test for vulnerabilities and produce a report detailing the results.

Identity spoofing, misconfiguration, password guessing tools

Even if systems have no known vulnerabilities from published CVE lists, they may still be vulnerable if misconfigured or if passwords or encryption techniques are weak. Password and encryption cracking applications have several ways of attempting to break into systems. One way is to use brute force, attempting every possible key within a given keyspace.

A quicker alternative is a dictionary attack which uses a list of strings commonly used for passwords, or a list of passwords extracted from previously compromised systems. Many systems will force a minimum number of seconds between login attempts, and will lock a user out if more than a given number of incorrect passwords are attempted. If these measures are not in place, compromise can occur.

In the case of encrypted communication, if a system uses a weak cipher, or a key that is too short, then encrypted traffic which is intercepted can be decrypted. This is particularly true for wireless communication systems. The use of distributed or cloud-based systems to provide the computational power to brute force complex passwords (Yong-Lei and Zhi-Gang, 2015) means that encryption systems previously considered secure can now be cracked for a relatively small financial outlay.

Tools which target wireless communications, such as Aircrack-ng, are available in the Kali Linux distribution. The interception and decryption of network communication may reveal login accounts and passwords which can then be used to gain access to systems. The most widely used tool for intercepting and analysing network traffic is Wireshark. Wireshark can capture live traffic or display previously captured traffic. If the appropriate private key is installed, Wireshark can also decrypt traffic from encrypted HTTPS or SSL sessions.

Password attacks may also be done offline. If a file containing encrypted passwords can be obtained, then this may be subjected to an offline attack, which does not involve the original system from which the encrypted password was obtained. This enables the password cracking to proceed undetected. Examples of files which contain encrypted passwords are the Linux /etc/shadow or /etc/passwd files, Microsoft SAM (Security Account Manager) registry hives and Cisco configuration files. 'John the Ripper' is a password cracking tool included in Kali Linux.

Application vulnerability testing tools

As more services become internet-enabled and ubiquitously available, the number and complexity of these services increases. Online systems often involve complex client-side scripting and on the server side have access to executable code, databases and authentication systems. As this complexity increases, so does the likelihood of the introduction of vulnerabilities.

A number of categories of tools exist which may help the penetration of online applications. Proxies, such as Web Scarab, intercept requests and may intercept, display and modify data between the client and the server. Web crawlers or 'spiders' can discover and list or copy the entire contents of a web application, and analysers such as nikto or w3af will test for known vulnerabilities.

The Open Web Application Security Project (OWASP) is an open community focused on improving the security of software. OWASP maintains a list of the Top 10 most critical web application security risks, which it describes as 'a broad consensus about the most critical security risks to web applications' (OWASP, 2017). These risks are generalised – for example, at the time of writing, OWASP risk A1 is 'Injection', which describes a generic process of introducing unexpected data to an interpreter, which may trick the interpreter into breaching normal security. OWASP itself provides an open-source framework which tests for these vulnerabilities: the Zed Attack Proxy (ZAP).

Burp Suite from PortSwigger Web Security is a similar commercial tool. Such tools may be configured for passive scanning, which will not attempt to modify requests or responses, and should therefore be safe to use in a penetration test of a production environment. Active scanning will attempt to use known injection attacks against targets, and may potentially disable or cause unexpected behaviour in the target systems. Many penetration tests will specifically exclude such attacks from their scope. However, being restricted to passive scanning may severely limit the ability of the test to expose vulnerabilities.

One of the most prevalent vulnerabilities is that of SQL injection (Clarke and Clarke-Salt, 2009) in which an attacker enters SQL statements and characters where the application is expecting a normal text response from the user. This code is passed by the web application to the database system, where its successful execution can cause the output of data not normally available to web users, or even the manipulation of tables and data within the database system. Web application tools differ in their level of automation and use. Some tools require only a URL, and will automatically investigate and test all embedded links within the web application responses from that URL. Other tools may require the tester to select links and choose the tests and probing strings manually.

One penetration testing technique which can be used in a wide variety of situations is 'fuzzing': this is the process of sending intentionally invalid data to a product in the hopes of triggering an error condition or fault. These error conditions can lead to exploitable vulnerabilities (Sutton et al., 2007). Fuzzing can be used against protocols, applications and services, and may range from simply hitting random characters on a keyboard, to sending data generated by a tailored application. Peach,[1] Spike (distributed with Kali) and Protos (a suite developed by Oulu University Secure Programming Group) are examples of software designed specifically for fuzzing (Baker, 2014). As fuzzing may cause failures in the target system, it is likely to be determined as out-of-scope in testing of production systems. If such tests are determined necessary, they could be performed against a test copy or dummy system, so that production systems are not harmed.

Comparison, evaluation and rating of penetration testing tools

Studies cited in Holm (2012) compare vulnerability scanners, but as there is a wide range of penetration testing tools for different purposes, it is difficult to achieve a clear comparison of tools. Penetration testing tools may be selected according to computer magazine ratings – for example, *Cyber Defense Magazine* (*CDM*) publishes a list of around 100 companies and products as their 'Infosec Award Winners' (CDM, 2017), but the large number of magazines, products and evaluations available makes this a difficult task. Market penetration or sales statistics may also give an indication of which tools to choose, although such statistics are difficult to find.

Companies such as NCC Group (www.nccgroup.trust) or Info-Assure (www.info-assure. co.uk) offering penetration test services will often also provide white papers, technical advisories or research papers, which may help in the selection of penetration testing tools. They may also publish information about the tools they use on sites such as LinkedIn (NCC, 2017).

While tools may automate many of the tasks involved in penetration testing, there is always scope for the creative individual to perform manual testing. A fully automated tool-based attack is unlikely to discover all vulnerabilities, and Austin et al. (2013) found systematic manual testing was most effective at finding design flaw vulnerabilities. The engagement of credible and certified penetration testing organisations brings the valuable experience of the penetration testers, who have applied their craft in a variety of contexts, and who bring a wealth of knowledge to the test which goes well beyond the ability to run a particular testing tool.

SUMMARY

This chapter has described some of the tools and techniques that can be used for penetration testing. Different tools and techniques are used in the reconnaissance, enumeration and exploitation phases of a penetration test. The scope of a penetration test should determine whether active or passive techniques may be used, bearing in mind that passive-only scanning may severely limit the effectiveness of a penetration test. Tools and techniques include port scanning, vulnerability scanning, password cracking, decryption, web crawling, code injection and fuzzing. Comparison of tools is difficult, and many testers and testing organisations will use a suite of tools with which they are already familiar.

REFERENCES

Allen, L., Heriyanto, T. and Ali, S. (2014) *Kali Linux: Assuring Security by Penetration Testing*. Birmingham, UK: Packt Publishing Ltd.

Austin, A., Holmgreen, C. and Williams, L. (2013) 'A comparison of the efficiency and effectiveness of vulnerability discovery techniques'. *Information and Software Technology*, 55 (7), 1279–1288.

Baker, S.D. (2014) 'Fuzzing: A solution chosen by the FDA to investigate detection of software vulnerabilities'. *Biomedical Instrumentation & Technology*, 48(s1), 42–47.

Barros, A. and Chuvakin, A. (2015) *A Comparison of Vulnerability and Security Configuration Assessment Solutions*. G00290479. Stamford, CT: Gartner Inc.

CDM (2017) Infosec Award Winners. *Cyber Defense Magazine*. Available at: www.cyberdefensemagazine.com/2017-cdm-infosec-award-winners/

Chiem, T.P. and Yan, W.Q. (2014) 'An overview of penetration testing'. *International Journal of Digital Crime and Forensics (IJDCF)*, 4 (6), 50–74.

Clarke, J. and Clarke-Salt, J. (2009) 'What is SQL injection?' In *SQL Injection Attacks and Defense*. Burlington: Elsevier. 1–26.

CREST (2017) *A Guide for Running an Effective Penetration Testing Programme*. Available at: https://www.crest-approved.org/wp-content/uploads/CREST-Penetration-Testing-Guide.pdf

Daintith, J. and Wright, E. (2008) Computer Misuse Act 1990. In *A Dictionary of Computing*, 6th edn. Oxford, UK: Oxford University Press.

Faircloth, J. (2016) *Penetration Tester's Open Source Toolkit*. Rockland, MA: Syngress.

Holm, H. (2012) 'Performance of automated network vulnerability scanning at remediating security issues'. *Computers & Security*, 21 (2), 164–175.

Kaur, M.G. and Kaur, N. (2017) 'Penetration testing: Reconnaissance with NMAP Tool'. *International Journal of Advanced Research in Computer Science*, 8 (3), 844–846.

Mell, P. and Grance, T. (2002) *Use of the Common Vulnerabilities and Exposures (CVE) Vulnerability Naming Scheme*. NIST Special Publication 800-51. Gaithersburg, MD: National Institute of Standards and Technology.

NCC (2017) NCC Group, June 2017. Available at: https://www.linkedin.com/company/ncc-group

OWASP (2017) *OWASP Top 10–2017: The Ten Most Critical Web Application Security Risks*. Available at: https://www.owasp.org/images/7/72/OWASP_Top_10-2017_%28en%29.pdf.pdf

PTES (2017) The penetration testing execution standard. Available at: www.pentest-standard.org/index.php/Main_Page

Storms, A. (2006) 'Don't trust your vendor's software distribution methodology'. *Information Systems Security*, 14 (6), 38–43.

Sutton, M., Greene, A. and Amini, P. (2007) Foreword. In *Fuzzing: Brute Force Vulnerability Discovery*. London: Pearson Education.

Tripathi, A. and Singh, U.K. (2010) 'Towards standardization of vulnerability taxonomy'. *2nd International Conference on Computer Technology and Development (ICCTD), 2010*. IEEE, pp. 379–384.

Wai, C.T. (2002) *Conducting a Penetration Test on an Organization*. Bethesda, MD: Sans Institute Information Security Reading Room.

Yong-Lei, L. and Zhi-Gang, J. (2015) 'Distributed method for cracking WPA/WPA2-PSK on multi-core CPU and GPU architecture'. *International Journal of Communication Systems*, 28 (4), 723–742.

11 GOOD PRACTICE FOR PENETRATION TESTING

Felix Ryan

Penetration testing can be done well or done badly; this chapter explores how to do it well. We will cover what could be tested, some common testing methodologies that could be used, the documentation typically used to commission penetration testing, and the documentation resulting from the exercise itself.

WHAT IS MEANT BY 'BEST PRACTICE' AND 'GOOD PRACTICE'?

Best practice is the broad term used by technologists to describe the best possible way of completing a task or overcoming a problem. The term suggests that there is a guidance document or manual somewhere that sets out the 'one true way'; however, this is often far from reality. The exact definition of what best practice means in a given situation is often debatable and is mired in the context of the challenge at hand.

It is easy for best practice to become an overwhelming beast, expending effort on ever-increasing levels of detail to make the task at hand perfect in every way. However, when it comes to penetration testing, it is far more important that the test is completed and, based upon the results, the necessary corrective actions are performed, rather than attempting to design the perfect testing programme. With this in mind, it is often better to require 'good practice', as this can enable the testing programme to achieve great things, without the unending pursuit of perfection.

Good practice, within the management context of penetration testing, means maximising the results for the budgetary limits and other constraints you are working within. To achieve this, ensure that pragmatism is in mind, for example, by working through the following overarching tasks:

1. Work with asset owners and map the entire attack surface.

2. Either use an existing risk analysis or perform a very quick risk analysis of each of the assets.

3. Prioritise the assets by the level of risk perceived.

4. Do not delay – commission an appropriate test of the highest priority target.

5. Present the summary of findings at the highest level in the business.

6. Secure budget for correctional activities and testing the next highest priority target.

7. Take a breath – and repeat...

Good practice activities for penetration testing practitioners occur between points 4 and 5 above and will vary depending on what type of exercise has been commissioned. Choosing the right type of testing is fundamentally important to getting the right job done, as it does not matter what good practice the practitioner puts into place if it isn't the right work in the first place. The main levels of testing services are: commodity; consultative; and full-spectrum Red Teaming.

Commodity testing services are about time and cost efficiency, which predominantly involve automated testing and will discover flaws considered as 'low-hanging fruit'. Consultative testing services will strive to understand the target's context, how the target actually works in the background, and will discover flaws that are only discoverable by putting all of the understood elements together. Full-spectrum Red Teaming builds on consultative testing, encompassing the entire spectrum of the organisation in one exercise; thus drawing on the flaws present on one target to attack another target.

There are some elements of good practice that all levels of testing services should have in common. For example: establishing clear and concise testing boundaries; establishing which in-scope systems are fragile and may experience difficulties following aggressive testing techniques; and ensuring the test is a fair representation of the system under scrutiny, whether that be regarding methods of sampling, or ensuring that no other security system gets in the way which could produce false-negatives.

BUILDING ON THE TESTER'S EXPERIENCE

Commissioners of consultative tests can lean heavily on the penetration tester to provide guidance and advice about how the penetration test will go, and how to get the most from it. They should expect advice regarding the breadth and depth of test coverage, what the results actually mean and ways that the testing programme can be improved in the future. They will probably also want advice on what corrective actions are possible, and how to fix the identified issues. After all, the penetration tester has invaluable knowledge of potential corrective actions as they have probably seen similar situations before, and they will have knowledge about how best to thwart their hacking efforts next time. This is a fairly common desire; however, there are a few problems with this.

First, defending and attacking computer systems take two very different skillsets and mindsets. There will be overlap, but the attackers are best placed to educate the defenders in how the attack was completed, not in the extreme detail of the configurations and methods of preventing the attack from happening again. Once the education is finished, the defenders should be able to perform the analysis required to determine the best course of action.

It is worth taking a moment to think about the consequences of asking the penetration tester for specific corrective actions though, as the tester might have a conflict of interest if they answer. Such a conflict of interest exists if the penetration tester ends up testing the work that they have been instrumental in implementing. This is similar in concept to a gamekeeper also being a poacher – the two roles can't work together. As a result, most penetration testers attempt to maintain objectivity by helping with everything other than actually fixing the problem. Typically, the advice provided by the tester will be high-level, won't include any product recommendations and will be more specific about any known pitfalls or possible undesired outcomes, rather than the way that it can be fixed. That said, sometimes there is only one way to fix the problem, in which case it is quite common to be given links for further reading online; for example, specific vendor guidance. Beyond this, any further advice may introduce bias into the testing process and will result in a loss of the objectivity provided by the penetration tester which is essential to the role.

The issue here, though, is that most organisations do not just want to be told that they have a problem – they want the solution as well. Understandably, this objectivity can be very frustrating, and can even damage the relationship you have with the tester. One of the best things to do in such a situation is to make it clear to the tester that there will be a rotation of penetration testers for the next time this particular target is tested; that way, they can feel less inhibited and give more specific advice. Although commissioners of penetration tests probably still won't get product recommendations, it is always a good idea to test the solutions being suggested before putting them live. Generally, it is a good rule of thumb to employ separate 'poachers and gamekeepers' – that way, there can't be a conflict of interest.

PENETRATION TESTING METHODOLOGIES

Penetration testing methodologies come in two main forms: a high-level approach to discovering and testing for vulnerabilities and weaknesses; and a definitive list of all the types of vulnerabilities and weaknesses that are known to exist. These two forms have significant differences when used to complete a penetration test. The most notable examples of these two forms are the Open Source Security Testing Methodology Manual (OSSTMM; Herzog, 2010) and the Open Web Application Security Project (OWASP) testing guide.[1] The OSSTMM is a guide to those commissioning the test as well as to those executing the test but it leaves the specifics to the organisations and individuals involved to determine significant details about the tools and tests to be completed. The OWASP Testing Guide provides very specific details about the test actions that should be taken.

Penetration testing methodologies can be quite contentious. This is because some penetration testers see methodologies as constraining and an affront to their creativity when it comes to their expertise and tradecraft. Equally though, it could be argued that it is only through the use of industry-accepted methodologies that commissioning organisations can be sure of what they are getting and how it compares with any other penetration testing exercise. A good penetration tester naturally follows the good practice that is outlined by high-level methodologies. They fundamentally understand how to simulate threats, how to develop attack strategies and execute those attacks. If there is confidence in the penetration tester, having a detailed methodology is likely to be something that does not need to worry you too much. Similarly, the more prescriptive penetration testing methodologies can be a great checklist for penetration testers to ensure they have covered everything they should have, but experienced penetration testers will not need to lean on these so heavily.

It has been argued that detailed methodologies are a continuation of the trend for penetration testing to become commoditised. Commoditisation is a double-edged sword, in that it makes penetration testing more accessible, in a number of ways, to the large numbers and variety of organisations that require these services. Some individuals voice concerns that the other side of commoditisation, however, is that it assists inexperienced penetration testers to operate fraudulently within the industry who are unable to detect complex vulnerabilities. As such, it is important for the organisation to use a methodology that is proportionate to the situation and appropriate for the entire context of the penetration testing exercise. This proportionate approach appears to be supported by the UK's National Cyber Security Centre (NCSC).[2] The guidance that the NCSC publishes advocates that each testing company has a defined and documented testing methodology[3] which requires certain testing and reporting elements be present in testing methodologies, but doesn't prescribe the details of those elements. This allows the penetration testing provider to work within their own constraints and based on their own expertise and experience.

All penetration testing methodologies have at their heart a drive for a minimum quality standard, consistency and strong coverage. These are clearly desirable qualities and are what gets rightfully pushed by the standards and compliance bodies; however, the potential negative effects that overly detailed and prescriptive methodologies may have rarely get discussed. The following points should be considered when deciding to what depth a methodology should go:

- A detailed methodology could reduce the opportunities and motivation for the penetration tester to use their expertise. This could occur if the requirements of the methodology encourage use of basic tools and techniques and therefore allow for a poor job to be completed. Or perhaps, the methodology requires significant effort to achieve ancillary tasks while not actually getting results from the testing itself.

- A detailed methodology could well raise the minimum standard, and it might well result in consistent penetration test results, but that is the **minimum** standard, and may not be the standard deserved by the sensitivity or magnitude of the system and organisation being tested.

- Consistency and a minimum standard might still be a useful requirement, for example, if the organisation is paying for less-experienced or junior consultants and they want assurance that a minimum level has been achieved, or perhaps if two products are being compared before one is to be chosen and implemented.

In theory it would be possible to write a penetration testing methodology that solves all of these problems and forces a high-quality, consistent test to be completed with strong coverage. However, such a methodology would be time-consuming and difficult to achieve. It could be that the organisation can have their consistency without losing that expertise-led investigation and get the best of both worlds. Unfortunately, this approach fails to realise that penetration tests are almost exclusively time-bound exercises and it is often not possible to satisfy both of these qualities. The organisation must understand these trade-offs and choose the approach based on its requirements.

There are circumstances where having a detailed methodology isn't optional. Perhaps the organisation has a client-assurance, compliance or legal reason for mandating a particular penetration testing methodology or level of depth that a methodology must achieve. One such example would be where the organisation is required to be compliant with the Payment Card Industry Data Security Standard (PCI DSS).[4] In such a case, the sales process should have identified this and the test provider will be allocating penetration testers that know how to work with the requirements. The good news is that most requirements to follow a methodology, including PCI DSS, are relatively flexible, stating that the methodology must be 'industry-accepted'. There are a few caveats here, because for example, PCI DSS does specify some small but very significant parts of the testing methodology, such as what is in scope and that boundary tests must be completed.

In the case of PCI DSS, the penetration testing methodology is the responsibility of the organisation being tested. That doesn't mean the organisation can't have assistance in creating it, but it does mean that the penetration testers are not responsible for validating that it will achieve the desired compliance goals. Even though the methodology is made specifically for a particular scope, that doesn't mean it can't be an industry-accepted methodology. In practice, the methodology must achieve industry acceptance by being able to stand up to scrutiny and critical evaluation. The onus is on the organisation being tested to take responsibility for its methodology because PCI DSS recognises that each environment is different and it is best known and understood by those that operate it. This is obviously a good idea as it should prevent any gap in coverage; however, in practice, many organisations struggle creating the methodology on their own and may enlist the assistance of the PCI QSA (qualified security assessors) or penetration tester. Expect to add a day or two, or maybe longer depending on the size of the environment, where assistance is taken from the QSA or the penetration testers before the penetration testing exercise.

DOCUMENTATION BEFORE, DURING AND AFTER A PENETRATION TEST

In this section we will look at the documentation and reporting activities that should be completed at various stages throughout a penetration testing lifecycle. This will include documentation that is needed for the commissioning process, final authorisations so that testing can get under way and in what form the exercise will be reported back to stakeholders.

Exercise build-up (before)

Exercise requirements questionnaire
Many testing consultancies like to formally try to capture the test requirements and the size and type of the exercise before they do anything else. Sales people particularly like this as it gives them a structure which they can follow while still getting the information required by the testers. It also means they have an excuse to communicate with the prospective client which inevitably means they can apply the art of relationship building. Smaller companies might not bother with this stage as the tester might be directly involved with the client from the beginning, in which case, they will understand more than a scoping document could record within a half hour conversation.

This is a stage that is not to be confused with the formal penetration test scope. Often the information assimilated at this stage will be used as part of that scope, but it will also try to collect information about the nature of the service which will help the provider when estimating the amount of time and effort that will be required to complete the work.

The proposal
Also known as a quote or formal test scope. This document sets out what the testing vendor is going to provide, exactly which systems or set of systems is in-scope, when and how long the service will be, the approximate outcomes and, finally, the cost. If there are any specific data safeguarding requirements they may be documented within the proposal or the contract. For example, the penetration testing vendor might keep evidence for a set period of time, or store it with certain security controls.

The contract
This is a standard business contract in most ways, though there will be some extra bits of note. Mainly, the additions are present owing to the fact that the activities carried out as part of a testing exercise are illegal to perform. According to the Computer Misuse Act 1990 there are four associated criminal offences:

> 1) unauthorised access to systems; 2) unauthorised access to systems with the intent of committing or facilitating further offences; 3) the unauthorised modification of computer material; and 4) making, supplying, or obtaining articles for use in breaking into computer systems.[5]

To perform any modern testing services, a tester will almost certainly break all four.

With 1) it can be argued that it is very difficult to give permission for the tester to access something when the method of access and the specifics of what is being accessed cannot be defined until after the exercise, and worse still, that the recipient of the exercise does not understand the tasks being carried out.

With 2) lateral movement is a very common tactic among real attackers and should be simulated whenever appropriate; as such the tester is aiming to commit further acts of hacking.

With 3) simply by using a system the user makes changes to computer material, performing invasive tasks such as a penetration test can make much larger changes.

With 4) most penetration testers come fully armed, either with tools and exploits acquired from the internet, or with tools and exploits they have created for specific purposes and vulnerabilities, or indeed create tools and exploits based on the systems which they find themselves attacking.

To make this more complex, there is no distinction in the act which allows information security professionals to perform the activities prohibited by the law. To make this legal problem go away, there should be a section within the contract that references these laws and specifies that the signing party agrees to indemnify the testing consultants for the purposes of performing testing services.

Authorisation to test form
It is common for this special law-avoiding part of the testing contract to be extracted into a stand-alone agreement as, in most circumstances, this will need to be re-signed

for each exercise, showing an ongoing understanding from the client and to tie this understanding to a specific exercise.

Exercise briefing (during)

Payment Card Industry (PCI) penetration testing methodology
The PCI council now requires organisations being tested as part of a PCI compliance effort to have this document and use it in relation to penetration tests. Strictly speaking, this document should be provided to the tester and sales people by the client in order to ensure that they receive the correct testing, and to confirm the scope of work. It is not uncommon, though, for the test service provider to help the client understand what is required of this document, and to help them write it at the beginning of a penetration test programme.

In this situation the testing parts of the exercise will be shorter than originally designed, or the bill will be larger owing to the extra time spent on the work. It is also important to realise that the penetration tester may not be qualified to advise on the testing methodology: it might be advisable to get this document signed-off by the PCI QSA as, ultimately, this is the individual who must be convinced that the penetration testing was adequate.

Target list
This usually only applies if the target is public or resides on shared infrastructure. The testers need to make sure they are conducting their tests against systems that belong to the client organisation. Depending on the details of the test, this might not be required at the very beginning of the programme: for example, the first stages might be reconnaissance. Once the tester is ready, they might submit their reconnaissance findings and get the client to compare the actual scope with their discovered scope and confirm any differences.

Alternatively, if reconnaissance is not necessary, the tester may require a confirmation of scope at the start of the exercise – even if this has previously been discussed. This is because enterprise IT systems are increasingly fluid in their design, particularly since the advent of cloud computing. A final target list that confirms the scope of the test also prevents the tester inadvertently testing a bystander.

Notification of vulnerabilities
The people responsible for commissioning penetration tests can be quite nervous about the outcomes, as can the penetration testers and the penetration testing consultancies. A common scenario is where clients ask to be notified of vulnerabilities the moment they are identified. Unfortunately, this can be quite disruptive to testing, particularly when consultants have a limited amount of time. The easiest, though slightly risky, option for the penetration tester is to simply carry on with the task at hand and wait till the formalised reporting period. The designated time in a penetration testing exercise for reporting is often at the end of the penetration testing exercise. The client and the penetration testing company may find this unacceptable, depending on their respective risk appetites. Lots of penetration testers also don't want the responsibility of knowing about issues that have not been reported to the client and that could be easily exploited at any moment, but find that the time pressures on the penetration testing exercise make it difficult if not impossible to report findings earlier.

In the majority of circumstances, a balance must be struck which identifies which criteria of vulnerabilities are reported upon discovery, and which are kept until the normal reporting schedule. For example, an agreement could be made that only vulnerabilities of 8.0 and above on the CVSS (Common Vulnerability Scoring System[6]) are reported immediately. This scheme has its own challenges though, as to be able to comply with this agreement, the penetration tester would have to calculate the score of every vulnerability as they go along.

Scoring or determining the qualities of vulnerabilities as they are found is an administrative task and any such task breaks the flow of penetration testing. Disruption to testing can impair the quality of the results which should be avoided where possible, but also more likely means that these tasks simply get forgotten in the heat of the moment. Experienced penetration testers have a gut feel about where a vulnerability's score or other determining qualities lie, which will guide them to whether they need to take action or not. Furthermore, some vulnerabilities are very obviously at one end of the severity scale and so need little thought to determine if they deserve client attention. If you have faith in the professional qualities and experience of the penetration tester, it may be better to have a loose arrangement in place that leans on their experience about whether or not a given vulnerability requires immediate notification.

To make matters more complex, when there is the discovery of something serious, it is all too tempting for organisations being tested to want to immediately take corrective action. However, the discovery and exploitation of some vulnerabilities expose additional flaws and items of concern. If corrective action is taken it may not be possible to discover such additional flaws and as a result the organisation may end up remaining vulnerable in some form without knowing it. This means it is vital for careful consideration to be made about how to proceed if a vulnerability is reported.

Exercise debriefing (after)

The report
This is ultimately what the client pays for. It is a document that should reveal all the skeletons in the closet and tell it like it is. Reports differ according to the exercise conditions and the depth of service commissioned: some reports are a table of results, others are just an executive summary, and others still, demonstrate all the tactics, techniques and procedures used in order to obtain the results of the exercise. The decision about reporting will be borne out of the motivations behind the penetration test; for example, client assurance, internal audit, project and product development, and so on.

Presenting the report

Given that the report is the most valuable part of the exercise to the client, make sure the delivery of the report is understood. It may be important to get more than just an email; for example, it might be beneficial to get a debrief meeting where the contents are discussed and where questions can be asked; and that debrief meeting can be more effective when it happens in person or in front of the team responsible for corrective actions.

Vulnerability scoring the report will probably involve some form of severity, risk or vulnerability ranking. Consider any specific requirements for this element of the report. For example, does it need to use the CVSS? It might do if you have a client that expects such a scoring system for its understanding and use, or if the report needs to comply with regulatory or other contractual requirements. Different scoring systems take different amounts of time, so this might add to the cost of the exercise.

Some clients find vulnerability scoring difficult to understand and to appreciate. Interestingly, there seems to be equal measures of clients asking for the ratings to be increased versus those asking for them to be decreased. Almost invariably, the cause for the drive to change the score of a vulnerability is rooted in whatever political event has led to a security testing exercise to be performed. It is worth asking questions about scores that are not understood; however, I would caution those who are trying to change a score to ask themselves the question – why am I trying to change this? When there is an answer to this question, be open and honest with the tester as they may be able to help in any number of ways.

Evidence and appendices
It is possible for the testers to gather a large amount of data during their activities. Some of this data might be useful when trying to perform corrective actions. For example, it is possible to get copies of usernames and passwords that were cracked when subjected to cryptanalysis.

Think carefully about evidence and how it needs to be treated. There are several factors to consider:

- Should the test service provider destroy all data and evidence collected? If so, how soon after the test programme has completed?

- Are there any uses for the test evidence by the teams that means the company needs to be given a copy of it?

- Is it wise for the data to be kept by anyone, for example copies of people's payslips or other personal data (there may be conflicts of interest)?

- How dangerous is the data? For example, having a list of everyone's username and password means that until those users change their password, whoever holds that data could be held to blame for any wrong-doing that those accounts are associated with.

- If the data is useful, but the risk is above a comfortable threshold, is there another way of getting the same benefit? For example, could an alphabetically sorted list of the usernames that had their password cracked, and an alphabetically sorted list of the passwords that were discovered be suitable? This way, trends can still be seen, but the usernames and passwords are disassociated from each other, making the data less dangerous. Alternatively, does the evidence need redacting in places to protect the individuals? For example, if a cache of passport scans is found, should the names and other personally identifiable information be removed before they are entered into any report or appendix?

- How should evidence be presented? Would a raw copy of the data be most useful, or perhaps a catalogued appendix?

Meaningful impact

Evidence can be used within reports to demonstrate impact. The selection of evidence to do this needs to be in relation to the objectives of the exercise and the context of the organisation, and ultimately it needs to reflect what was actually obtained as opposed to hypothetical achievements. There is nothing more effective at rendering the results of a test inert, than a hole being picked (no matter how inconsequential) in the evidence submitted within a report.

PENETRATION TESTER TRAVEL AND BEING AWAY FROM HOME

Owing to the current worldwide shortage of penetration testing consultants, there is a very strong chance that the testers will have had to travel a reasonably long distance in order to attend the site of the test. This has several knock-on effects both on the testing exercise and on the tester personally:

- General fatigue – no one, including testers, ever sleeps as well in a hotel as at home.
- Bad back (i) – testing consultants end up packing every piece of equipment 'just in case'.
- Bad back (ii) – meeting room furniture is fine for a couple of hours, but not for days on end.
- Extra cost – the client will likely end up paying for extra time, covering travel and their expenses.

To help the tester maintain the best level of efficiency, it might be appreciated if it is indicated that, at their discretion, the maximum amount of testing that can feasibly be performed remotely is preferred. This will allow testers to recuperate with family and friends in the evening, catch-up with the post that inevitably arrives when they are away from home and eat normal, 'real' non-restaurant food (a surprisingly common desire for travelling testers).

TEST TEAMS VERSUS INDIVIDUAL TESTERS

The testing exercise might be large enough to justify the use of a small team. Wherever possible, this is recommended, because the testers will be able to discuss problems with each other. Having the ability to talk directly to another tester enriches their abilities and enables them to come up with creative concepts and potential avenues of attack. Better still, when in a team, all this verbal communication can be completed without having to redact the content for fear of giving away client details, which might be required with other forms of communication such as plain-text emails.

Don't worry if the exercise is just too short to justify the cost of a small team. Where this is the case, exercises tend to be of a low enough complexity that no significant benefit would be achieved by working in a team anyway.

THE CLIENT BEING INVOLVED IN THE TEST

Penetration testing is quite an exciting concept for managers and techies alike, particularly when it is new to an individual or to the organisation. This can often lead to a desire to watch every moment and have regular meetings and debriefs and hear about the latest exploits. As a tester, this is flattering, but is also a worry. Inevitably, the sales process has determined a number of days to complete a job and, regardless of how that number of days was established, the job needs to be completed to deadline. Unfortunately having an extra shadow or techie-soulmate can make this challenging because the discussions that take place absorb a surprising amount of time.

The truth of the matter is that penetration testing can actually seem rather boring to spectators. That is because a large proportion of what a tester tries to achieve does not actually work; after all this is the point: testing to find out whether something can be used in an unexpected way and most of the time it cannot. Hacking is not like it is depicted in television shows or movies, there is no magic button that immediately lets the adversary 'in'. Sitting alongside the penetration tester while they are working could well just make them feel nervous and probably gives them stage-fright. It is a common observation among techies that the moment anyone is watching, the typing abilities of the person at the computer evaporate.

Even if the testers don't have a permanent companion while they are working, having regular debriefs with them can disrupt their flow and make it difficult to remember exactly where they were up to. It can also interrupt at a critical, time-sensitive moment as the penetration tester is always going to give the client the attention they request. Both ultimately absorb precious time. It is rare to find a penetration test where there is no more testing to be done or new attack methods to theorise. It gets worse than this, though: if a penetration tester is being asked to give an update every couple of hours it can come across as betraying a lack of confidence in their abilities. From personal experience, it is often a very positive sign when the customer wants to join in with the geekiness; however, it is possible to have too much of a good thing. To get the most out of the penetration testing exercise it is a good idea to formally schedule one or two debriefs as a task at the end of the exercise. For example, have a debrief just for the organisations' techies and a second one for management. This is where the tester can walk you through everything they have found, or give live demos, and answer any questions as well as present new ones. The two different audiences will be interested in different parts of the process and have different questions, so to be time-efficient it may be a good idea to separate the two conversations. There may also be sensitive questions that are best asked with few others to hear. These debriefing decisions will be entirely down to the operational characteristics of the organisation, though the experience of many penetration testers shows that, wherever possible, a good balance of stakeholders and a healthy level of openness breeds better results.

It is really important to maintain enough distance so that the objectivity of the penetration tester isn't compromised. Penetration testing exercises are usually performed to give the client organisation or third parties a level of assurance on the system's information security. If the organisation is too involved in the penetration testing that objectivity quickly erodes, which seriously diminishes the value of the testing exercise.

Larger organisations might want to formalise their involvement in security tests in advance, but smaller organisations may not see any requirement to do so. There is no right answer, as each organisation will know what its own requirements are and the context of this particular penetration testing exercise. However, it is vital that the implications of being actively involved are understood so that the adverse effects are compensated for or accepted where necessary.

HEALTH AND SAFETY

Penetration testers are humans too. Health and safety is really important for all employees, contractors and consultants regardless of where they usually work and what they usually do. This applies just as much to penetration testers as anyone else and it doesn't matter who is legally responsible. At an absolute minimum, the client has a moral responsibility to ensure that the penetration tester is well looked after and not put in any short-term or long-term danger. Don't just think of this as whether or not the penetration tester needs to wear a hard-hat in any warehouses, but also whether the desk and the environment is suitable where the penetration tester will be for the majority of the time.

SUMMARY

In this chapter we started off by examining the difference between 'best practice' and 'good practice', and how good practice is almost certainly good enough. We identified that while best practice is an honourable aspiration, it can be very difficult to achieve and as a result may slow down or stop a penetration test from happening. We then continued with this theme, looking at ways of making a penetration test more successful by harnessing the pragmatic. We discussed how the client being heavily involved in the test is not necessarily conducive for getting good results and that instead a balanced approach is much better. We also looked at what good practice means when it comes to the various elements of paperwork that will be required and created throughout a penetration test exercise.

REFERENCE

Herzog, P. (2010) *OSSTMM 3: The Open Source Security Testing Methodology Manual.* ISECOM. Available at: www.isecom.org/mirror/OSSTMM.3.pdf

12   ROLE AND COVERAGE OF REPORTING

Gemma Moore

Following any penetration test, you will generally receive a formal report from your penetration test provider. In this chapter, we will explore the role and purpose of a penetration test report, the type of content that will be included and how to use the report content most effectively within your business. A penetration test report, when well-written, will illuminate your technical risks, providing clarity around the business context of the vulnerabilities present with pragmatic advice to treat the risks. Understanding what you need from a penetration test report, and how to interpret report content, can greatly improve the efficacy of your technical assurance activities.

PURPOSE OF REPORTING

In almost every circumstance when a penetration test has been commissioned, a penetration test report will be produced and presented at the conclusion of the engagement. The broad objective of any penetration test report is to provide the commissioning organisation with a detailed description of its current risk profile across the scope of testing.

Internally, the way in which the penetration test report is used and interpreted will influence how much value for money is realised from the penetration test. There are several broad ways in which a penetration test report is used by organisations who commission technical assurance programmes; for example:

- To provide evidence of compliance to external third parties or customers, for contractual, legislative compliance or regulatory reasons.

- To understand the current risk to the business present within a system or application, to feed into internal risk acceptance discussions.

- To provide tactical short-term remediation advice to reduce risk present within a system or application at the time of the assessment.

- To identify patterns or trends in technical vulnerabilities which might relate to wider process failures to be addressed at a strategic level.

- To validate that internal controls and procedures are functioning as expected, and cannot be circumvented.

- To assess or manage a known threat or specific threat adversary.

The overarching objective of the owner of a penetration testing programme is to use technical assurance to assess the risk to the business, so that the risk can be managed and reduced. In reaching this objective, you need to understand, interpret and translate the penetration testing reports that you receive so that:

- The appropriate business context is applied to the risks identified, including an overlay of business risk onto technical vulnerabilities, and the application of wider contextual intelligence to the report, based on a narrow scope.

- Both narrow-scope technical vulnerabilities and wider-scope process failures can be identified and classified.

- A remediation and risk management plan can be produced which takes into consideration all the contextual information you have, including the penetration test itself.

- The right stakeholders internally are apprised of what they need to do following a penetration test, why they need to do it, how they should go about it and how urgent the action is.

DISTRIBUTING REPORT CONTENT TO THE RELEVANT AUDIENCE

Every project, network, application or other component which is subjected to penetration testing will have its own stakeholders with some interest in the outcome of the penetration test. These are likely to include:

- The overall senior risk owner within the business, with responsibility for managing risk appetite and risk tolerance globally within the business.

- The nominated system(s) or asset(s) owner(s) with whom overall responsibility for the system under test lies.

- The project team responsible for developing the system or application, particularly where project-based assurance is the driver for the penetration test.

- Where the penetration test is part of a regular ongoing assurance programme:

  - infrastructure support teams;
  - application development teams;
  - application support teams;
  - customer support teams and helpdesk functions.

- Budget holders, who will need to approve or reject expenditure related to risk management activities following the penetration test.

- Any third-party service providers who are involved in the management or provision of the system or components under test.

A penetration test report, in its raw form, will likely not be suitable for consumption by all constituencies of interest within your organisation. To help in the creation of an effective mitigation and risk management plan, it is important that results are digested and processed to present the relevant information to each constituency.

It is not likely to be cost-effective to commission an external penetration testing provider to create tailored reports for each constituency of interest, though this may be easier to accomplish with internal teams. For most businesses commissioning penetration tests from external suppliers, an internal process is needed to make sure that reporting information is delivered to the right personnel in the right format.

The senior risk owner for the enterprise needs to understand, from the penetration test, what the risk is to the confidentiality, integrity and availability of relevant data assets managed by the systems under test. This interpretation of the risk will often need to be informed by the business context of the system under test and any relevant business impact analysis which has been conducted. They do not need to have access to the technical details of every technical vulnerability.

Conversely, application development teams and infrastructure support teams will require all relevant technical detail from the penetration test report so that they are able to understand the vulnerability, replicate it within their test environments, properly scope the effort required to develop fixes for issues identified and implement these effectively. The overall business risk context is less important for these groups.

A third party, providing implementation or management of part of the systems under test, only needs to understand the vulnerabilities relating to the scope of their involvement in the project; providing them with additional information about risks outside their control is unnecessary.

Unnecessary distribution of information about your security vulnerabilities, such as that contained within a penetration test report, is undesirable as the information could fall into the wrong hands and be used against you. It is always best to think about restricting access to this information to those you trust.

A prerequisite to getting this step right is to have a clear understanding of the stakeholders involved, and what information they require in order to be able to fulfil their roles properly. It may be helpful to complete a RACI (responsible, accountable, consulted and informed) matrix for each stakeholder or stakeholder group when organising the communication of penetration testing results from a report to ensure that this information is captured. The sponsor of the penetration test can then capture the relevant extracts of information for dissemination to the relevant groups.

A responsibility assignment matrix is a device which outlines who is responsible, accountable, consulted and informed (RACI) when it comes to completing tasks or receiving deliverables within a business. In the context of a penetration test report, for example, the person responsible for implementing the systems assessed would require all information about a particular vulnerability, including technical details, if they were to remediate the issues. Those accountable for the affected business unit may need to know the type of risk identified, but may not require the technical details of exploitation.

COVERAGE OF REPORTING

Before conducting a penetration test, or selecting a penetration test provider, it is important to think about the sort of information which will be useful to you within a penetration test report, and how you would like it to be presented. In this section, we cover the types of content you will likely find in your penetration test report, the limitations you may wish to consider, common reporting metrics and trend analysis techniques that can be helpful in the long term.

What a penetration testing report should cover

Reporting formats themselves vary widely between different penetration test providers; when choosing a provider, reviewing the format of the report which will be produced is a useful step to undertake to ensure that the penetration test report will meet your requirements.

If using internal teams to conduct your penetration tests, you may be able to make very specific requests in terms of report formats; you might not have the luxury of full customisation with external testing teams. Always discuss your reporting requirements with your provider – most suppliers will work flexibly with you to ensure that the report you receive gives you the information you need in the format you require it, and if you desire tweaks to formatting and information presentation this can usually be easily accommodated. If your requirements are substantially different from an external supplier's standard report, however, you may find that custom report formats will come at a cost; factor this into your negotiations accordingly.

Whatever the type and scope of the penetration test commissioned, a penetration test report will normally contain these elements:

- A representation of the technical vulnerabilities present within the scope of examination.
- Several scoring metrics for each technical vulnerability identified, and therefore a risk associated with that technical vulnerability.
- Recommendations for remedial action and mitigations to either remove each technical risk entirely, or reduce it to a manageable or acceptable level.
- An executive summary, aimed at a non-technical audience, which aims to explain the risk.

A penetration test report may also include any or all of the following:

- An opinion on business risk, rather than technical risk, for each issue that has been identified.
- An analysis of patterns and trends in the risks identified, aimed at identifying areas where a strategic approach to mitigation is recommended – effectively, a 'root-cause' analysis.
- Advice in terms of prioritising mitigations for the issues identified during the engagement.

- An opinion on aggregate risk whereby individual technical risks may be combined during exploitation to greater adverse effect.

- Areas where additional investigation, either internally or by further testing, is recommended and the reasons for making these recommendations.

The core content for the report will be a technical description of every vulnerability, weakness or exposure encountered during the penetration test.

Generally, for each technical risk identified, the tester will provide a broad description of the issue and its type, together with a detailed technical description of the specific instance of the vulnerability as encountered during the penetration test in the environment under test. As part of this dissection of the detailed vulnerability, the tester will usually also provide an interpretation of the business risk introduced by the technical vulnerability.

Providing such an opinion on the business risk relies upon the knowledge of the penetration tester as it relates to business operations. Many factors can influence how complete this business risk interpretation will be, including the type of penetration test commissioned and the information provided to the tester before and during the engagement. Obtaining the best results in terms of business context and business risk placement within a penetration test report (particularly when commissioned from an external party) relies upon providing the tester with a good background to the business operation and details of the security requirements for the system.

Most vulnerability reports will provide concrete recommendations for the mitigation of each vulnerability identified. Where a fix for the issue is well-defined and the issue itself is constrained in scope, these recommendations are likely to be tactical, short-term, one-time fixes which can be implemented relatively swiftly. Where issues identified are systemic, or symptomatic of wider process failures or design flaws, recommendations may be far more strategic in nature, in which case short-term workarounds may be recommended while long-term changes to the environment can be planned and implemented. Sometimes third-party links and references will also be included to provide further information about the vulnerability identified, or about the appropriate risk treatment which should be applied.

As with many formal business documents, an executive summary is usually included in a penetration test report. This summary will be aimed mainly at a non-technical audience and will provide some overarching guidance to senior personnel within the enterprise as to the present risk posture of the system under test, a description of the broad business impacts encountered and an opinion of the priority actions for remediation within the environment. Where the tester has noted patterns in the root cause of the issues identified, the executive summary will often include strategic recommendations for long-term improvements in information security.

It may be that during a penetration test certain test cases could not be fully explored, or indicators of potential vulnerability were identified which could not be validated by the tester during the engagement. In these cases, the report may contain recommendations for further testing, or for further investigation internally to rule out additional vulnerabilities.

An important part of the report is a section which contains the details of the engagement, including a description of the scope and environment under assessment together with details of the testing approach taken and the names and qualifications of the testers involved in the engagement. As part of this description of the engagement, the report should contain details of any constraints or limitations that applied to the testing. Understanding what threats have not been assessed can be as important to risk management efforts as understanding the risks which have been definitively identified. As an example, there may be certain test cases for which a cloud service provider will not give authority to test, or areas of functionality which could not be accessed by the user accounts provided to the tester. In these instances, noting the exclusion of such test cases within the report is crucial for the enterprise to understand what potential threats remain unaccounted for.

If a penetration test is being conducted for compliance reasons, there may be specific reporting guidelines which should be followed. For example, in the UK the National Cyber Security Centre runs a penetration testing scheme called CHECK which applies to many penetration tests carried out by public sector organisations. All penetration test reports generated under the CHECK scheme must meet a detailed list of requirements specified by the NCSC and available on their website.

For retailers wishing to gain compliance with the Payment Card Industry Data Security Standard (PCI DSS), any penetration test report generated to support this compliance would need to address all of its requirements for penetration testing, including a section on testing of network segmentation where this has been implemented. If all relevant areas are not covered correctly in the report, it may be insufficient to withstand a compliance audit. When commissioning the penetration test, it is important that specific reporting requirements relevant to compliance programmes are therefore captured and communicated to the penetration test provider.

Common reporting metrics

As part of the presentation of each vulnerability in the report, the provider is likely to include a number of metrics. As with reporting formats, reporting metrics in penetration testing can vary widely, but the metrics that are commonly applied to vulnerabilities within the industry are shown in Table 12.1.

The values in Table 12.1 will likely be provided against some form of quantitative scale, which then maps to a qualitative 'risk' rating. The way in which these are calculated should be explained and documented within the report.

In addition to general metrics in Table 12.1, which are susceptible to subjective interpretation, the penetration test provider may also call upon external scoring systems such as the Common Vulnerability Scoring System (CVSS). CVSS aims to provide a standardised, objective scoring system for technical vulnerabilities based broadly on the concepts outlined above. Correct scoring for CVSS, except at the base level, again requires that the tester has extensive information about the environment and requirements for confidentiality, integrity and availability in the context of the business.

While industry scoring systems such as CVSS are very useful, they can sometimes fail to provide a meaningful score for risks identified during a penetration test. Where the risk

Table 12.1 Vulnerability metrics as applied (examples)

Metric	Description
Impact or severity	This is a measure of how much damage could be caused if the vulnerability were successfully exploited.
	The definition of 'damage' is usually dependent on the tester's understanding of the security requirements of the environment under assessment and any relevant business impact analysis which feeds into the engagement.
	As an example of how dependent this metric can be on context, consider a financial trading system which must be constantly operating with low latency in order to allow trades to occur in a timely manner versus the same organisation's corporate website. If a penetration test identified the same denial of service vulnerability in both systems, the impact on the business of this vulnerability within the financial trading system will be far higher than within the corporate website due to the potential financial damage that would be incurred by an interruption in trading.
Exploitability or likelihood	Exploitability and likelihood may be considered together or separately. Generally, these metrics aim to put a numeric value on how likely it would be for a technical vulnerability to be exploited, and the ease with which it could be exploited.
	This metric will usually consider information such as what threat actors are known to target the system in scope and their technical capabilities, as well as publicly known information about the vulnerability. Factors such as whether the vulnerability can be exploited over the network, and whether authentication is needed for exploitation will also be considered.
	Intelligence about the business environment is useful to the tester in positioning this metric accurately. For organisations with little in the way of valuable data and no known advanced threat actors targeting them, for example, a vulnerability which has no publicly available exploit may have a very low likelihood of exploitation. The same vulnerability identified within an organisation which is known to be under active attack by advanced teams may have a moderate or high likelihood of exploitation simply because of the threat actors known to be involved.
Risk	Each technical vulnerability is generally assigned a risk value, based upon both the impact and severity of the issue and the exploitability and likelihood of exploitation. In some cases, the risk will be a numeric value but usually it will be mapped to a broad category, for example: negligible, low, moderate, high or critical.
	A penetration test provider will be able to provide you with the details of how they calculate risk.

is a consequence of the inherent design or function of the system under assessment, a CVSS calculation could be meaningless. Where the risk resides, because of business processes, outside of the technological influences, applying standardised industry scores may not be possible.

Vulnerability classification systems and taxonomies may also be included within the reporting metrics during a penetration test, such as:

- The Common Vulnerabilities and Exposures (CVE) project is a dictionary of common names for publicly-known cyber-security vulnerabilities.

- The Common Weakness Enumeration (CWE) project aims to provide a taxonomy to standardise the classification of software weaknesses; aligning all software weaknesses identified to a standard such as this facilitates onward trend analysis by ensuring consistent categorisation.

- The Open Web Application Security Project (OWASP) Top 10 is often used to highlight the positioning of web application vulnerabilities and provide a reference point for developer research and education.

- The Common Attack Pattern Enumeration and Classification (CAPEC) scheme aims to provide a consistent taxonomy for referring to the types of attack which adversaries undertake, and broad classes of recommendations to address these attack patterns.

Part of reviewing and choosing a penetration testing provider will be asking which metrics they use, and ensuring that these metrics are suitable for your purposes.

Trend analysis for individual businesses

Each penetration test report typically covers a single system or application in isolation; an overarching analysis and interpretation programme is often required to provide good intelligence about patterns and trends. As mentioned above, each penetration test provider will use their own reporting formats. In many cases, a penetration testing programme may involve the use of multiple penetration test providers across different time periods and different target scopes. Standardising and interpreting results is a key challenge for penetration test programme owners in such circumstances.

Where a penetration test provider has worked on a particular target scope over multiple penetration tests, they will have access to historical data regarding the history of the engagement and can comment on whether tactical and strategic remediation efforts have been effective, and where patterns of vulnerability provide evidence for areas where processes and procedures should be improved. Where suppliers of penetration testing are rotated, this historical information will not necessarily be available to the penetration test provider for reference, and hence the trend analysis and intelligence around it would need to be provided by the business itself following receipt of the penetration test report.

Trend analysis across all penetration test reports is also extremely valuable internally in terms of identifying wider business issues and efficiencies in terms of remediation work that could be required.

When a programme of penetration testing is commissioned, establishing the framework for longer-term trend analysis of all reports will save effort over the long term. Consideration should be given to which metrics are desirable to track during the analysis, and how this information should be collected. Choosing standardised metrics and taxonomies to include within the trend analysis is key to this step. The use of standardised taxonomies (CVE, CWE, OWASP, CAPEC et al.) when recording penetration test results into any form of trend analysis platform allows consistency in comparison between different systems, and between different result sets over time.

Standardising risk values for penetration test report findings can be more difficult. If these tools are not available to you within your business, you can often gain useful intelligence by adopting a consistent data entry format into a spreadsheet or database and producing graphs of the relevant information, combined with thinking about the questions to which you would like answers; for example:

- What are the commonalities across different systems or applications in terms of the vulnerabilities identified? Do these commonalities suggest that there is a failing in a particular process globally; for example, in software patching? Are there global controls that can be adopted to address a global risk?

- If your organisation has different development teams working on different applications, how do the vulnerabilities identified within each project differ? Are there weaknesses in one development team which do not seem to be present in the others, or different standards adopted across the different teams? Are there cross-training opportunities to be used?

- Are there areas where remediation work is failing on a repeated basis? What could be causing this failed risk reduction work?

- How long does it typically take your organisation, from identification of a risk which requires removal, to successful removal of the risk? Is this an acceptable window of vulnerability?

If you have a preferred format for entry into any form of trend analysis system (such as CSV, spreadsheet or XML), your penetration test provider may be able to provide you with results in that format in addition to the standard penetration test report; this should be discussed with them when selecting a provider.

SUMMARY

A good penetration test report will help you understand your current exposure, and give you clear advice about how to treat the risks identified. It will provide relevant information for different stakeholders, including a high-level business risk overview for senior management and full technical details for your operational teams. It is important that you carefully consider what you want from a penetration test report when choosing a provider. You should be confident that you are au fait with your provider's reporting methodology and terminology so that the report can be properly interpreted once it reaches your desk. Taking the time to put together some long-term trend analysis tools may provide you with root-cause analysis over time and hence help you become more proactive at tackling technical risk throughout your business.

13 INTERPRETATION AND APPLICATION OF REPORT OUTCOMES

Gemma Moore

Once you have received your penetration test report, you need to decide how to use it and what to do with the information therein. In this chapter, we look at the usefulness of debrief meetings, the importance of applying business context to the technical risks identified, and how to integrate findings into bug trackers and ticket managers.

ON DEBRIEFS

When interpreting a penetration test report, it is important to understand the limitations of written communications that surround the production of a report written by an external penetration tester. In this context, considerations to be borne in mind include the following:

- The test consultant who has performed your penetration testing is not likely to have a full understanding of the business context for the system or application in scope. This means that their interpretation of the technical risks in the business context is likely to be incomplete.

- The scope of a penetration test is often confined to isolated systems, networks or applications; as such, the penetration tester will not have a full understanding of the wider context in which the environment under test sits. Without a full understanding of the wider technical context for the components in scope, the technical risk presented within a report may not reflect the actual risk to the business from the existence of the vulnerability when factors affecting other systems are taken into account.

- A penetration test is generally a time-constrained exercise which provides a point-in-time assessment of a single set of in-scope components. This means that the results of the penetration test and the contents of the report can only be considered valid for the specific environment tested at the time it was assessed, and under the circumstances of the engagement. Applying the results of a penetration test report to systems over time or across different related environments, therefore, necessitates a robust change control mechanism.

With these limitations in mind, a debrief meeting following the completion of the draft report is extremely helpful to all parties. During a debrief meeting, there is an opportunity for the penetration tester to have a two-way discussion about the wider business context with stakeholders in more detail, gaining a fuller understanding of the actual impact of the issues identified.

It is quite likely that in some cases technical teams may not fully understand the vulnerabilities present; a debrief discussion gives these personnel a chance to properly discuss the vulnerability directly with the tester. Not only does this information transfer mean that onward remediation planning is likely to be more effective, but this type of education can prevent recurrence of vulnerabilities.

Similarly, the debrief meeting gives the tester an opportunity to ask questions about the business environment which provide additional background to the technical vulnerabilities and inform the risk. These discussions may also reveal the ultimate scale of aggregate risk of joining multiple vulnerabilities together and therefore provide valuable input to the way individual vulnerabilities are prioritised in remediation.

It is also a golden opportunity to discuss possible remediation strategies and alternatives with the security tester.

There is no hard-and-fast rule about how a debrief should be performed, and the format will often depend on how much communication your operational teams had with the penetration testers during the assessment, and on the breadth and scale of the risks identified. The most effective debrief sessions will be tailored to the requirements of your business. In some cases, a short conference call may be all that is needed to ensure that all stakeholders have a good grasp of the risks and how to start work on remediation. For larger-scale, complex projects, a series of meetings with different stakeholder groups may be needed, possibly with dedicated executive-level presentations and low-level technical workshops with operational teams.

INTERPRETING REPORTS AND CIRCULATING KEY FINDINGS

A penetration test report can vary widely in size and complexity. Most penetration test reports will be exception-based, meaning that rather than containing exhaustive details of each and every test case and result during the assessment, the content is focused on those areas identified as presenting risk. As a result, two penetration tests with similar-sized target scopes in different organisations could result in two vastly different report lengths, where one target scope was well-implemented in terms of security and the other was not. The length of a penetration test report, however, is never a good indicator of the return on investment (ROI) in conducting the testing; trend analysis can provide better ROI measures.

In order to interpret a penetration test report properly you must have a good understanding of the security requirements of the system or application. If you have business impact analyses for these systems or assets, these will inform your understanding of the risks present in the report; for example:

- Is confidentiality of the system in scope important?
- Is integrity of the data stored necessary for the business?
- Is availability the most important criterion?
- What is the worst thing that could happen to the system and how much damage would it cause to the business if it happened?

- What other systems rely upon the items in the scope of the penetration test and how could they be affected in the event of a breach?

The overall risk appetite of the organisation and the acceptable level of risk for the system or application in scope of the penetration test will also inform the way in which an identified vulnerability is addressed. If an identified risk cannot be accepted, it will usually need to be reduced, through a fix, through the implementation of compensating controls to reduce the risk or in some other manner. Quantifying the risk within the context of the business may be difficult, but correlation with business impact analyses will aid in this assessment.

Using this understanding, the penetration test report should be examined with a critical eye and each technical vulnerability prioritised in terms of its importance for business operations. To do this, the impact to confidentiality, integrity and availability of each risk must be assessed. Table 13.1 provides an example of the way in which different vulnerability impacts may affect the importance of a reported technical risk to an affected system where only one key priority exists for that system.

Table 13.1 Vulnerability impacts on risks (examples)

Key system priority	Example of vulnerability impact		
	Denial of service	Remote code execution	Unauthorised information disclosure
Confidentiality	Not important	Very important	Very important
Integrity	Not important	Very important	Not important
Availability	Very important	Only important if the availability can be compromised this way	Not important

In reality, the assessment of the importance of an individual technical vulnerability impact is likely to be far more nuanced and guided by detailed business impact assessments. Systems and applications rarely only have a single key priority, and these are often not absolute. A short period of downtime can often be tolerated well; minor information disclosure will not be catastrophic in many cases.

Remediation of risks identified during a penetration test will often not be trivial. Where a penetration test report identifies systemic or complex flaws, a complete fix for these risks may be time-consuming and costly. In some cases, risks identified may be inherent to the business process in scope, or the design decisions made during the development of the application or system and may have to be accepted.

Full remediation of vulnerabilities may therefore not be possible nor desirable in all cases – mitigating risks completely might, for example, have an adverse impact on the usability of systems which would impact wider business goals. Conversely, there may be 'quick wins' within a report which can substantially reduce the risk overall with very little investment (for example, applying critical patches to vulnerable systems). For more complex issues, or those which would have a knock-on effect on other systems or business processes, a discussion between stakeholders will be needed to ensure that the business risk of the issue is fully understood and to determine a way forward. This is often something that can be initiated during the penetration testing debrief meeting, and continued during general business activities.

Decisions about whether to treat risks identified will generally come down to an assessment of the cost to fix versus the maximum business impact of the risk (as determined by a business impact assessment), taking into consideration the usability consequences of any treatments applied. Identifying the 'quick wins' from a penetration test and disseminating these directly to those operational teams responsible for implementing the remediation for action is a good way to provide short-term risk reduction.

Even where the risk identified is low, if the fix for the issue is trivial it should be considered for inclusion in system or application maintenance procedures. For this to be successful, change management processes need to allow for such requests following the penetration test.

As we have already seen, the full penetration test report may not be appropriate for all stakeholders. The findings of penetration tests are generally sensitive information and, depending on your organisation's culture and security requirements, you may feel that restricting access to the findings of a penetration test to a need-to-know basis is sensible. Equally, in some cases, providing too much information to a department could risk slowing down progress by overwhelming them with irrelevant information.

With an understanding of the role of each stakeholder group, key information can be extracted and circulated efficiently. Having information about system ownership for all constituent assets within the scope of the penetration test will allow the relevant findings related to those assets to be disseminated directly to the owners responsible for review. The high-level executive summary from the report may be appropriate for a wider audience. The senior risk owner for the business may only require visibility of the high-level risks identified during the engagement and their metrics.

It is not in the interests of an external penetration testing provider to exaggerate or tone-down the risks identified within the target scope of the assessment, and most external providers will generally refuse to compromise their impartiality when it comes to reporting on risks identified objectively. Having said that, if there is a specific business goal behind a penetration test (for example, gaining budgetary approval for particular works, or providing assurance around a particular security requirement), commentary within the penetration test report can often be tailored to your business's needs so that the desired outcomes can be achieved.

INTEGRATING REPORTING INTO BUG TRACKERS, TICKET MANAGERS AND MANAGEMENT TOOLS

In order to ensure effective remediation, risks identified during a penetration test will often need to be integrated into other systems, such as change management and ticketing systems, bug trackers and management tools. The report in its raw form is likely to consist of a PDF document with details of all risks found and a large amount of technical detail. As previously mentioned, the report, given its content in respect of the vulnerabilities present in the target scope and the ways in which these can be exploited, is also sensitive in nature.

When integrating this information into other systems, you should consider how much information is appropriate to include in each information management system, the audience for that information management system and any wider security implications. Consider whether you need to enforce need-to-know access to the details of these risks or add secondary controls to this information when you send it to other systems – such as additional encryption or password-protection.

 Vulnerability details from a penetration test report, in the wrong hands, could be used to attack you.

Development teams looking to implement bug fixes will require the full details of any risk identified with their application. In these cases, providing a high-level description of the risk and remediation advice will likely not be sufficient for the development teams to work effectively. The information risk owner for the business, using a governance, risk and compliance (GRC) management tool, likely does not require information about the individual technical details of each risk in order to perform their tasks effectively. In these cases, including the full technical details of each risk within the GRC management tool would likely be excessive and would unnecessarily disclose information into this external system.

Integration should also consider where responsibility for implementing or managing remediation work lies. In a penetration test report, the findings are often grouped by affected target; as such, one finding may have multiple systems or applications which are affected by the risk. If actions for addressing the risk across different systems need to be assigned to different operational teams, or different system owners, the same finding from the penetration test report may need to be included within a ticketing system multiple times, with different assigned teams to action the required response. Failure to correctly assign remediation work separately to the relevant teams could lead to a fix being marked as complete by one team, when a second team has not yet completed the activities they would need to action in order to close off the risk in a second affected system.

Some risks identified might require a multi-stage remediation process; for example, where a technical fix is required at multiple stages within an application code base and these parts of the code base are managed by different teams. Again, failure to understand this when creating the tasks in any bug tracking or ticketing system may result in incomplete remediation being logged as 'complete'.

For bug trackers, particularly, it is important to include sufficient information in these trackers to allow the development and testing teams to replicate the circumstances that led to identification of the risk and to provide details from the penetration test report which explain how to re-test the vulnerability. The inclusion of this type of information will allow development and test teams to ensure that their remediation efforts have been successful.

UNDERSTANDING THE FULL IMPLICATIONS OF VULNERABILITIES

A penetration test report should be presented so that the risks identified, and their wider implications, are clear to all relevant stakeholders, including technical operational teams and executive risk management teams. Where information in the report is unclear, or not understood, your penetration test provider will generally be happy to expand on the vulnerability identified or incorporate feedback into an updated report. Some technical vulnerabilities identified during penetration tests may be complex and difficult to understand; for this reason, debrief meetings are invaluable as they allow many such uncertainties to be addressed directly with the stakeholders concerned.

A penetration test report will always include tactical fixes for short-term risk management and mitigation. It will often also include longer-term recommendations for changes in policies, processes and technologies which may help to prevent a recurrence of the risk in future.

Once a penetration test report is analysed, you may also find that many of the risks identified spring from related root causes – inadequate patching of client software, for example, or a lack of developer education. For example, where susceptibility to a known vulnerability has been identified on a computer under assessment, a recommendation to apply the specific software patch missing would be a short-term tactical fix. Longer-term, your report may include recommendations that suggest the patching process as a whole should be reviewed to prevent other software patches from being missed in the future.

A mistake often made by businesses in acting on penetration test reports is to focus heavily on the tactical short-term remediation to reduce the immediate risk to the business, and failing to address the longer-term strategic issues which led to the introduction of the risks in the first place. This is often due to limitations in budget or investment, though it is also observed in businesses where penetration testing is commissioned on a per-project basis with no overarching penetration testing programme for the whole organisation. Understanding the strategic problems within your business, and addressing these at the root cause, will generally reduce the spend on security over time; prevention is almost always better than cure for most information security risks.

Consistent trend analysis across all penetration test reports is key to understanding these strategic issues, and generally it is useful to have a person or department with visibility of all penetration test reports in place to ensure that this strategic intelligence is properly gathered. For businesses without the resources to achieve this, developing a strong relationship with the penetration test provider can help. Most external penetration test providers work with customers of a variety of sizes across many industry sectors, and are able to offer opinions and advice on strategic issues as observed during a penetration test – this is another reason why debrief meetings following a penetration test can be very important.

The trend analysis role typically sits within the remit of whoever is responsible for managing risk across the business, though it is not uncommon for such trend analysis activities to sit within the remit of technical or IT teams, or within those budgets. Organisations whose responsibility for penetration testing lies within operational technical teams can sometimes experience problems when looking to reduce the risks identified, as it can be difficult to gain executive buy-in to changes which need to be made in the wider business as a whole, or to gain sufficient budget to take remedial action when this needs to be obtained from operational budgets. For this reason, risk management is often more effective when it falls within a dedicated board-level remit.

A second mistake made by businesses in reviewing penetration test reports is to fail to take into account the impact of the risks identified to systems or processes outside the immediate scope of the penetration test. As an example, one system may be found during a penetration test to disclose the randomly generated ID numbers which are used to uniquely identify customer accounts to the business's customer service team, but no other information. A second system, outside the scope of the penetration test, may use the same unique customer ID number as a mechanism to identify an authorised customer when they log in, allowing access to sensitive personal data.

Security assumptions for the second system rely upon the unpredictability of the customer ID number as a control to prevent unauthorised access to the sensitive information. In isolation, the information disclosure identified during a penetration test of the first system may be tolerable to the business, and hence not included in remediation efforts. The result of this penetration test, however, invalidates a key security assumption made in the management of risk for the second system; that is, that the customer ID number cannot be obtained or generated automatically by an adversary targeting the sensitive data which is stored in the second system.

This is not an easy problem to address for many businesses. In an ideal world, full-coverage penetration testing would be conducted across all systems and assets within an organisation, with the penetration test team fully aware of all interconnects and dependencies between the different systems and applications under test. In the real world, such an exercise would be cost-prohibitive for most businesses and entirely impractical. Instead, success generally relies upon good communication between the penetration test stakeholders and the team conducting the testing, together with a robust risk management process which considers knock-on impacts throughout.

SUMMARY

Overall, the better the relationship and communication between the business stakeholders and the penetration testing team, the more effective and productive any penetration test programme is likely to be. Business-wide oversight, good internal communications and a good relationship with your penetration testing provider are the hallmarks of a successful technical assurance programme. When penetration testing is conducted as an isolated activity, within particular business silos or without high-level oversight and buy-in, the wider context for risks identified and patterns of process failure can be lost.

14 ACTING ON PENETRATION TESTING RESULTS

Jason Charalambous, Moinuddin Zaki and
Tylor Robinson

Once the outcome of a penetration test has been reported and delivered to the client, and the risks fully presented and discussed, there follows a 'remediation phase'. This is the most crucial element of the penetration test lifecycle where identified vulnerabilities are addressed in order to reduce or negate the impact they have on the business.

One of the primary reasons this phase is often not given enough attention is the perception or mindset of organisations that consider a penetration test programme as a box-ticking exercise; where the initial delivered report can be used as supporting evidence for various purposes such as compliance, a tender or an audit process, without understanding the adverse impact certain vulnerabilities will have on the business if not fully perceived and acted on appropriately.

Furthermore, an indication of a vulnerability on a certain asset may originate from an erroneous chain of operational procedures that are built on insecure or weak foundations and which – if not identified through a proper risk assessment – will introduce the same risk again when remediation is attempted. As an example, if a server contains a number of weaknesses that have been remediated, but resurfaced in other systems, a root-cause analysis should also be undertaken for other operational functions such as technical training, with a revision of the build configuration standard for such server deployments. This is required because these weaknesses will be inherited in future server enrolments as a result of staff unawareness or from an ineffective, standard automated process.

It is always a challenge to correctly assess broadly the interdependent components and processes affected by a vulnerability and its associated risk. It is important in the remediation phase for an organisation to create both a long-term and short-term remediation road map that will include:

- correct development of fixes;
- enforcement and deployment of fixes;
- testing of the applied fixes;
- required expertise and resources;
- associated costs;
- timelines and milestones.

To effectively address vulnerabilities, a successful vulnerability remediation programme must be able to plan the required steps effectively and efficiently, including assigning responsibilities to personnel, allocating the right resources and managing associated costs.

INTERPRETING RESULTS

When interpreting penetration testing results, a cool, collective approach should be taken that emphasises the prioritisation of remediating critical and high-risk vulnerabilities. It is advised that low-risk vulnerabilities are addressed at a later stage, especially when time is limited. This can be challenging due to the way that low-risk vulnerabilities are perceived as simpler or quicker to fix.

In situations where organisations have sufficient IT personnel, remediation strategies can be altered. In such events, based on the complexity of a vulnerability, suitable skilled personnel can be allocated consecutively to multiple vulnerabilities. It is important to note that even when a vulnerability has been rated as low risk, it should not be considered negligible from a security perspective.

A low-risk vulnerability is generally only rated as such because the likelihood and impact of exploitation is minimal at the time of assessment. This of course varies depending on newly available exploits or if it can be used in combination with other vulnerabilities that have the potential to lead to an organisational compromise. This combination of vulnerabilities is generally referred to as a 'chained attack path'.

By their very nature, vulnerabilities can be coupled, and the complexity of such associations can rapidly become incomprehensible. Penetration tests generally include attack paths; graphical representations that illustrate how one vulnerability can be chained to interconnect with multiple other vulnerabilities. The introduction of such visual aids for vulnerability identification have dramatically reduced the strain of keeping track of associated vulnerabilities.

Prioritising results

Not all findings are considered equal and some often pose a much larger risk to an organisation. The exploitation of high-risk vulnerabilities can often lead to the compromise of a company; as such the following factors should be considered in prioritising the remediation activities in order to formulate an effective remediation plan.

1. Importance of the affected asset
It is vitally important to understand the value, liabilities, costs and sensitivity of the affected asset to the business. This can be assessed by understanding its involvement and criticality in the business's operations and its interdependencies – including the data itself. Given an example of a domain controller that can issue and hold user

accounts – one organisation might assess only the server itself where people can authenticate in the network to do their job functions; while another might assess what information the authentication controls themselves serve to provide.

2. Impact on the business if the vulnerability is exploited

Every asset carries a different weight in regard to its involvement in the business operations, the data it holds, its interdependencies and the impact it will have if exploited. Such exploitation could lead to various different impacts as listed below, but not limited to:

- productivity loss;
- financial loss from productivity;
- fines due to legal and regulatory constraints;
- reputational damage;
- liability and competitive advantage.

3. How easy it is to exploit the vulnerability

Given the fact that a vulnerability has been identified, a notable factor to be considered is how pragmatic it is that it can be exploited and under what conditions (i.e. if there are available exploits, easy prerequisites or conditions to allow an attacker to exploit the vulnerability, time required for the attacker to successfully exploit the vulnerability, and so on).

4. What the threat landscape is, by considering the attack vectors

There could be multiple threats to an asset wherever a weakness has been identified. It is important to have a good understanding of these different threats, together usually called a 'threat landscape'. Each threat within the landscape can impact either the confidentiality, integrity or the availability of an asset. It's important to have an understanding of the threat landscape and the various paths that could lead to a compromise/breach.

5. The effort, resources and cost needed to fix the issue

Fixing a certain vulnerability requires proper planning, testing and implementation of a fix. This can be a very resource-intensive exercise depending on the scope of the assessment, the size of the organisation and IT personnel (in-house or outsourced) expertise. Often, when businesses outsource their IT infrastructure operations to a third party, the time required for them to fix vulnerabilities could be longer than expected (and depending on the management or contract, may come with additional costs).

Vulnerability risk assessment

A risk assessment (RA) is an important tool in the assessment of an organisation's asset exposure. It aims to identify the risk that is facing the organisation and takes into account the identified vulnerabilities, including the current threats. There are many quantitative and qualitative (or a combination of these two) risk methodologies and frameworks that can be used to provide a simplified understanding of the overall risk.

Qualitative analysis

Qualitative analysis is an approach in which the risk is calculated based on the probability of that risk being triggered with its associated impact. These types of assessment rely on people's context or expertise with the knowledge of the asset or process being assessed. Such risks often have relative scales or values (high, medium or low or 1–10) to display the level of severity, as this has no monetary or mathematical dependency. Using only this type of analysis may lead to biased results regarding the probability and associated impact rating, which can lead to non-pragmatic prioritisation of effort taken to address a risk.

Quantitative analysis

Quantitative analysis on the other hand deals with measurable data that are useful to express probability and impact values including the monetary loss for each threat, weakness and impact. As this type of assessment relies on mathematical formula calculations, it can be used for the benefit of controlling issues.

The framework and approach taken in risk assessment must be able to identify and describe the assets, threats and controls – including the impact and potential loss elements of these.

Vulnerabilities reported by the penetration testing provider will contain a risk rating and a measure of how easily they can be exploited, as the findings need to reflect pragmatic realities. These risk ratings need to be reviewed based on the impact they can have on the business and the types of processes that your business uses. Carrying out a RA helps in making an informed decision about the remediation steps, such as accepting or rejecting a risk and prioritising the actions (including any associated costs and resources required).

As it is practically impossible to fix everything at once, the risk assessment provides a metric of the types of risk that the organisation is facing, based on the outcome of the penetration test. The purpose of a RA is to enable organisations to view the different potential impacts of risks with regard to their business objectives, operations and reputation, which will result in more effective and appropriate resolutions. Based on these factors, an organisation can prioritise remediation activities.

ESTABLISHING A STRUCTURED REMEDIATION PLAN

A structured remediation plan outlines the follow-up strategy required to remediate issues identified from the penetration testing process.

Remediation activities

Remediation activities are a comprehensive collection of solution and test processes that outline the way in which an issue will be fixed. The ultimate goal of the remediation phase is to ensure that the risks posed by vulnerabilities are either completely removed by fixes or reduced to acceptable levels. There are different types of fixes that can be applied to remediate a vulnerability. They include the following:

1. Applying a certain patch and hotfix

Organisations or communities behind operating systems and applications provide regular patches and hotfixes when a security vulnerability is discovered in their products. Most of the time, depending on the product, an implementation guideline is issued together with the patch or 'hotfix', which makes applying a patch or a hotfix a straightforward process.

> The difference between a patch and a hotfix is that the patch is released in order to fix a known issue or weakness and the hotfix to immediately fix a very specific issue.

2. Upgrading an application or host

Sometimes a small hotfix or a patch might not be enough to fix a security flaw. Hence, a firmware upgrade or a version upgrade may be required to completely negate a certain vulnerability. Most leading IT vendors periodically upgrade their products to enhance various features, and to enhance the security. Major firmware or version upgrades come with changes (i.e. deprecation of certain features) that a company needs to be aware of (i.e. upgrading PHP5 to PHP7).

3. Reducing the attack surface

Services and protocols may have inherent weaknesses, especially in the way they are designed (e.g. FTP and Telnet), and these should not be used anymore due to their inherent risks. If there is no business need to keep the services up and running, they must be replaced with services with similar functionality, or a compensating control should be added to remove or reduce the impact of exploiting such a protocol.

When remediating vulnerabilities, security teams should attempt to identify and remove important entry and exit nodes that are interlinked with multiple other branches of the attack path. Once this link has been identified, administrative teams can start to act upon remediating vulnerabilities. This is referred to as 'breaking the attack chain', and when done correctly can lead to an organisation having a much smaller attack surface.

4. Fixing weaknesses in the code

Any in-house developed products and applications (e.g. company website or login portal) that usually serve only the organisation that develops and maintains them could be found insecure during a penetration test. In such scenarios, source code has to be revisited to address and fix the identified vulnerabilities.

5. Developing a new solution or redesigning the current solution

This is necessary where a flaw is identified in the core of an asset and which is inherited by other various process; for example, if a web application has been found vulnerable to multiple issues such as SQL injection, cross-site scripting attacks, missing proper access control functionality and so on. To fix issues like these, the entire application may require a rework or a redesign. Such a fix or remediation is usually the most resource-consuming option, where there is a need either to build a new solution or to redesign the current one.

6. Implementing a compensating control

Sometimes, a fix might not always be a solution. There could be many reasons for this, such as impracticality, costs, resource constraints or no timely available patch from the vendor, which makes it very challenging. In situations like these, efforts should be made to delay, detect or completely deter an attack that could exploit a vulnerability. A compensating control, also known as an alternative control, can be set in place to satisfy a control that may be deemed impractical or difficult to set in place. It must have a similar risk reduction to the actual fix to lower the risk to an acceptable level.

7. Completely removing the affected asset

Based on the identified vulnerability, a business decision can be made to remove the affected asset or service completely. As an example, this could be a server that is not in production and hence has been left unmaintained with security vulnerabilities but still resides on the company's network.

8. Sometimes, just accepting the risk

A risk assessment may indicate that the overall risk for a certain asset and its associated dependencies is low. Taking into consideration the possible solutions in this list, the organisation may decide not to act on a vulnerability, because the resources, time and costs may be higher than the value of the asset itself. However, it is strongly recommended whenever a certain risk is accepted that it is well justified, documented and revisited.

Applying changes or fixes within an IT environment is certainly not as easy as filling a small hole or applying a bandage to a wound. It is sometimes highly complicated: more akin to complex surgery than a bandage. Hence, the fixes need to be tested first in isolated mirrored environments (where possible) or on staging environments before being applied on the live production systems in an effective change control process. Fixes that have not been tested can result in severe outages, causing financial and reputational losses to the business.

Remediation strategy

A mature remediation strategy could ensure that similar vulnerabilities do not reappear in the future, which would save money on future remediation activities. A comprehensive strategy would lead to more secure baselines for solutions, which would allow further vulnerability risk assessments to focus on identifying more complex issues.

When defining a remediation strategy to fix a certain vulnerability, the following factors should be considered:

- Time, resources and costs required to plan the remediation. There will not be a single fix available for all the vulnerabilities that have been reported. Sometimes, a modification in the code of a system is required or a compensating control needs to be put in place. All interdependencies of the change should be captured in this phase in order to avoid any adverse disruption on other components. Moreover, the business needs to make sure that time constraints and resources required in planning, testing and applying the remedial activity have been considered.

- Time, resources and costs required to test the fix. Any changes that are planned have to be tested. During the testing of the fix, efforts should be made to make sure a certain fix does not open up a different attack surface or a security hole within the application or infrastructure.

- Time, resources and costs required to implement the fix. After successfully testing the fix, it should be scheduled to be rolled out to the production environment in a controlled manner. Efforts should be made to do this as soon as possible after a successful test through a controlled change management process.

An effective remediation strategy requires at least the following parameters for every item or vulnerability that has been identified:

- Timeline for all remediation phases (planning, deployment, testing).

- Associated costs of carrying out a fix. As an example, remediating a number of vulnerabilities in a custom-made application created by a supplier specifically for an organisation may require a substantial amount of work, and additional costs may be involved due to the way the contract agreement has been reached.

- Designation of individuals or teams that will be responsible in each of the remediation phases.

Allocating ownership

First and foremost, a dedicated team needs to be assigned the remediation tasks in order to carry out the fixes to the selected vulnerabilities in clear co-ordination with other relevant teams. The personnel overseeing the remediation phase should track the remediation progress at all stages, to provide a historical reference for the records:

- The testing and implementation progress of the fixes that are or have been applied on a particular asset including time frames.

- Other interdependencies that rely on the affected asset. These will come in very handy when there is an adverse impact or an incident reported, in case the fix has caused an unforeseen event.

- The outcome (successful or not).

- Personnel involved in the task.

Once all the remediation activities have been identified, they should be prioritised by the security team leads. After completing this step, it would be the ideal opportunity to present the action plan and feedback to the relevant teams. The teams should prioritise addressing their assigned activities to reduce the duration the associated vulnerability presents a risk to the organisation. Once teams have been debriefed, the team leads should communicate the expected time frame for remediation activities, based on feedback from the relevant teams. It should be noted that during the remediation process, risk could be re-evaluated or the remediation approach could change as the issue is explored.

The remediation plan should extend beyond only addressing vulnerabilities and should transition into a strategic lifecycle that focuses on creating strategies to reduce the likelihood that similar, organisation specific vulnerabilities are identified in the future. This transition should preferably only occur once the immediate risk – the affected technology issues – have been addressed.

PENETRATION TEST TIMINGS

It is important to measure how fast an organisation can classify and respond to vulnerabilities. Response time, as it is termed, has become increasingly important. It is the total time taken by an organisation to identify, classify and remediate a vulnerability. However, one has to measure the effectiveness of the remediation before confirming whether a vulnerability has indeed been remediated.

Due to the fact that penetration tests come in different flavours (i.e. have been executed from an external or internal perspective, been authenticated or unauthenticated and so on), it is strongly recommended for each organisation to set a framework or road map in place with a third party for such tests to commence at different time intervals, aiming at different components of the organisation – depending on the organisation's requirements and risk appetite. These frameworks should also cover post-breach activity scenarios or ongoing system migration from one provider to another. This framework should be defined as part of the strategic organisational objectives to ensure that the cyber risk is kept as low as possible.

Re-testing is another crucial step during the remediation phase. After applying the remediation steps to an asset, the business should plan on executing a re-testing process to ensure that the fixes are effective in plugging the vulnerabilities. Re-testing is a simple and effective way of gauging the progress made against the remediation plan. Generally, a re-test should only be performed on all vulnerabilities where fixes have been attempted. Different re-tests can occur on different time frames, depending on the severity of the vulnerability. Efforts should be made to plan the re-testing phase into short-term and long-term assessments; that is, including re-testing of the critical and high-risk vulnerabilities before assessing other medium- or low-risk vulnerabilities. As mentioned previously, everything that is deemed unacceptable needs to be resolved in a timely manner, as waiting longer periods will mean that a complete reassessment is needed. Due to an ever-changing threat landscape and vulnerability disclosure, a delayed tailored re-test on the affected component may not be sufficient to uncover new weaknesses.

An acceptable time for remediation can be determined by the nature of the issue. This is expressed more specifically as:

Severity of the vulnerability × Likelihood and impact of the vulnerability being exploited × Asset value

Vulnerabilities that are 'critical' or 'high' risk should be remediated immediately, but realistically it has been industry-accepted for these to be resolved within a month. Other medium-to-low risks – those that do not have any direct or indirect impact on the confidentiality, integrity or availability of assets – can be fixed within three months.

There are of course vulnerabilities that require more time to be completely resolved (i.e. migration to a new platform or re-writing core functionality of an application that has many interdependencies or an upgrade); here it is suggested to put mitigating controls in place to lower the risk to an acceptable level until a final solution is set in place.

SUMMARY

Penetration testing offers the opportunity to validate an environment's current security posture and to protect a business. By selecting the right scope and the right type of test, one can identify and remediate the identified security vulnerabilities. Far from being a stand-alone procedure, penetration tests need to be an integral part of the overall risk management programme. Always remember that true security is a holistic, overall approach that goes far beyond technical measures. Good security should be a culture within an organisation, based on a cycle of continuous improvement.

Acting effectively on penetration test results is of vital importance. This involves careful preparation of a road map for the required development and deployment of fixes, including the human resources and associated costs that will need to be involved. Equally important is the reassessment and verification that any applied security fix has the intended outcome, otherwise such processes must be repeated. Communication between all relevant parties and stakeholders in an organisation is essential and this lifecycle is an integral part of a continuous deployment programme to address business risks and act upon them.

NOTES

NOTE: All URLs were correct at the time of writing.

PREFACE

1. CREST website, 'About CREST'. www.crest-approved.org/about-crest/index.html

CHAPTER 1

1. BCS penetration survey, conducted in March 2017. The survey was sent to a collection of people who had expressed interest in this book in a previous survey sent in early 2016. Respondents included those who have applied penetration testing (25%), those who have organised penetration testing (25%), end-users (32%) and academics with an interest in penetration testing (<35%).

2. https://www.shodan.io/

3. https://www.latimes.com/archives/la-xpm-1989-06-13-mn-2300-story.html

CHAPTER 2

1. See https://wikileaks.org/ciav7p1/index.html

2. https://www.kali.org/

3. https://nmap.org/

4. https://www.metasploit.com/

5. The attack surface (or attack vectors) is the number of different entry points by which an attacker could try to penetrate a system. It is the sum of all entry points via vulnerabilities within a system.

6. See https://cve.mitre.org/

7. See https://www.pcisecuritystandards.org/

8. www.ncsc.gov.uk/articles/composition-check-team.

9. See www.first.org/cvss

10. See https://www.wifipineapple.com/

CHAPTER 3

1. Cloud providers will typically specify the scope and rules of engagement of penetration testing that clients are allowed to carry out. The kind of penetration testing will vary based upon the types of service to be tested. For example, Infrastructure as a Service (IaaS) services are likely to support extensive testing however the shared multi-tenant nature of Platform as a Service (PaaS) or Software as a Service (SaaS) services may limit or even prevent permission for penetration testing from being granted.

2. www.crest-approved.org/about-crest/

3. https://www.ncsc.gov.uk/scheme/penetration-testing

4. https://www.tigerscheme.org

5. https://www.thecyberscheme.org/

6. www.legislation.gov.uk/ukpga/1990/18

7. See https://www.legislation.gov.uk/ukpga/1974/37

8. Communication of the social engineering aspects of the penetration test should be kept to the minimum required to ensure the test remains effective whilst avoiding unintended alarm such as from calls to law enforcement, for example.

9. https://ico.org.uk/for-organisations/data-protection-reform/overview-of-the-gdpr/

10. https://ico.org.uk/for-organisations/data-protection-reform/overview-of-the-gdpr/breach-notification/

11. See https://www.itgovernance.co.uk/cobit

12. https://www.axelos.com/Corporate/media/Files/Glossaries/ITIL_2011_Glossary_GB-v1-0.pdf

CHAPTER 4

1. The ICO's Monetary Penalty Notice detailing the findings of the case cites, as one of the contraventions that led to the issuance of a fine, '18. (a) Boomerang Video failed to carry out regular penetration testing on its website that should have detected the error'. See https://ico.org.uk/media/action-weve-taken/mpns/2014300/mpn-boomerang-video-ltd.pdf

2. The phenomenon of IT being procured outside the IT department, even without their knowledge. Although this has existed for some time, it is becoming ever-more prevalent, with the increasing existence of cloud-based software as a service (SaaS) offerings.

3. An attack in which the availability (i.e. the 'A' in the 'CIA (confidentiality, integrity and availability) triad') of the system is disrupted, in order to prevent legitimate authorised users from having access to it.

4. A contraction of 'development' and 'operations'. The basic premise is that, through the use of greater degrees of automation and virtualisation, the divide between development (i.e. producing software) and operations (i.e. 'running' the resultant software) can be narrowed, or even eliminated entirely.

5. In software engineering, CI is the practice of merging all developer working copies to a shared mainline several times a day (https://en.wikipedia.org/wiki/Continuous_integration).

6. CD extends this concept even further, extending to actually delivering the (continuously updated) software to real users.

7. File integrity monitoring is a mechanism that uses hashing to identify which files, or parts of a given file, have been altered. In this context, it could be used to highlight which specific parts of a release have changed.

CHAPTER 5

1. https://www.cisecurity.org/critical-controls.cfm

CHAPTER 7

1. See www-history.mcs.st-and.ac.uk/history/Extras/Babbage_deciphering.html

CHAPTER 8

1. In this context, 'out of band' refers to attack vectors which occur outside the 'usual' channels, which might be readily available to an external attacker (and hence, an external penetration tester; operating under a black-box or grey-box testing model).

2. WebDAV – web distributed authoring and versioning; a protocol that extends http to offer facilities such as copying, changing and moving files on a web server.

3. 'Masking' card data refers to the practice of obscuring some or all of the data (typically, areas of the PAN – Primary Account Number), typically with a symbol such as an asterisk.

4. Requirement 11: Regularly test security systems and processes, PCI DSS V3.2, PCI Security Standards LLC.

5. Supervisory control and data acquisition (SCADA) is a control system architecture commonly used in industrial, manufacturing and utility contexts. It uses computers, networked data communications and graphical user interfaces for high-level process supervisory management, but uses other peripheral devices such as programmable logic controllers and discrete PID controllers to interface to the process plant or machinery (https://en.wikipedia.org/wiki/SCADA).

6. Voice over internet protocol. Although essentially IP traffic like any other, the nature of VOIP sharing many characteristics with voice calls can mean that systems used to deliver this fall outside the experience of typical, more traditional computer-oriented testers.

7. TCP/IP – transmission control protocol/internet protocol; an especially common suite of protocols governing both the internet and internal networks.

8. The shorter development cycles of these methodologies bring quicker (and often cheaper) potential for resolution than more traditional SDLC models, such as Waterfall.

9. OWASP (Open Web Application Security Project) is an open-source resource that seeks to address application security. One of its most notable outputs is the creation of a 'Top 10', a list of the '10 Most Critical Web Application Security Risks'. Available at: https://www.owasp.org/index.php/Category:OWASP_Top_Ten_Project

10. Some penetration test experts regard it as an ethical requirement to highlight if the architecture of systems in any way constrains the effectiveness of the test. This is not to suggest that testing is not worthwhile, or should not be performed, but rather that this deficiency should be expressly highlighted within the report. Where such architecture makes the system harder to maintain, perform more slowly or deficient in some other, 'not directly related to security' manner, some service providers view it as an additional 'value add' of a conscientious penetration tester to provide commentary on this, rather than something they're obliged to do.

11. Metasploit is a perennially popular penetration testing framework.

12. The ability to automate the process of testing is especially desirable in SDLC models geared up for rapid iterations between releases, especially in environments that begin to approach continuous integration, where it is not possible to manually test on a continuous basis.

CHAPTER 9

1. See https://www.cyberaware.gov.uk/cyberessentials/

2. See www.crest-approved.org/

3. See https://www.isc2.org/cissp

4. See www.isaca.org/CERTIFICATION/Pages/default.aspx

5. See https://ico.org.uk/for-organisations/guide-to-the-general-data-protection-regulation-gdpr

6. See https://www.ncsc.gov.uk/guidance/cloud-security-collection

7. See https://cloudsecurityalliance.org/

8. See www.CERT.org/octave/osig.html

9. See https://www.owasp.org/index.php/Category:OWASP_Application_Security_Verification_Standard_Project

10. See also https://www.ncsc.gov.uk/guidance/implementing-cloud-security-principles and https://ico.org.uk/for-organisations/guide-to-the-general-data-protection-regulation-gdpr

CHAPTER 10

1. www.peachfuzzer.com

CHAPTER 11

1. https://www.owasp.org/index.php/OWASP_Testing_Guide_v4_Table_of_Contents

2. See https://www.ncsc.gov.uk/articles/check-methodology

3. See https://www.ncsc.gov.uk/articles/check-methodology

4. See https://www.pcisecuritystandards.org

5. See https://www.legislation.gov.uk/ukpga/1990/18/contents

6. See https://www.first.org/cvss/

INDEX

www.ingramcontent.com/pod-product-compliance
Lightning Source LLC
Chambersburg PA
CBHW060137060326
40690CB00018B/3909